HANDBOOK OF
BAR CODING SYSTEMS

Document Network. Reproduced with permission of Texas Instruments, Inc.

HANDBOOK OF
BAR CODING SYSTEMS

Harry E. Burke

Under the aegis of the
Data Pathing Systems Division
NCR Corporation

VNR VAN NOSTRAND REINHOLD COMPANY
_____ New York

Disclaimer

Any program based on a cipher set should be referenced to the most up-to-date information supplied by the code-control organizations listed in Appendix C or to other standardizing sources.

Library of Congress Catalog Card Number: 83-23522
ISBN: 0-442-21430-8

Manufactured in the United States of America

Published by Van Nostrand Reinhold Company Inc.
115 Fifth Avenue
New York, New York 10003

Van Nostrand Reinhold Company Limited
Molly Millars Lane
Wokingham, Berkshire RG11 2PY, England

Van Nostrand Reinhold
480 La Trobe Street
Melbourne, Victoria 3000, Australia

Macmillan of Canada
Division of Canada Publishing Corporation
164 Commander Boulevard
Agincourt, Ontario M1S 3C7, Canada

15 14 13 12 11 10 9 8 7 6 5 4 3

Library of Congress Cataloging in Publication Data

Burke, Harry E.
   Handbook of bar coding systems.

   Includes index.
   1. Product coding. I. Title.
HF5416.B87   1984   658.5'64   83-23522
ISBN 0-442-21430-8

Preface

After a diffident history as a lightly regarded labeling technique, bar coding has blossomed profusely. This has happened because bar coding is finally recognized as the only printable machine language. That is, bar coding reproduces directly, in documentary form, the bit-streams of ones and zeros which are the basis for all digital computer languages. It is now a vital element in any program maximizing both the productivity of an organization and the effectiveness of its management.

Unfortunately, within this pervasive movement many implementing decisions actually compromise the potential of the bar-code art, making it more expensive to use, less versatile in application, and much less reliable than it could otherwise be. This has come about because those features which determine both print and read reliability are not well understood. For instance, most bar-coding schemes do not even take advantage of byte configuration features which have been used for years, by designers of digital computers, to move information with the maximum degree of reliability.

The purpose of this book is to highlight key bar-code issues and to place these issues appropriately within the twin context of technology and application. Here is a guide which an organizer of a bar-code program can use to chart his way through the morass of industry standards and commercial sales literature.

HARRY E. BURKE

In Acknowledgment

This material was developed under the aegis of NCR Corporation. During 1981 and 1982 the author visited more than one hundred discrete manufacturing facilities discussing these matters with their staffs. This document is, then, one individual's composite response to a broad range of applications and objectives. In addition, as may be observed by the illustration sources, many vendors to the bar-code market have been most generous with their ideas as well as their material.

However, in no way should the interpretations of the concepts outlined herein be considered a consensus. The bar-code art is undergoing significant change and, until it settles down a bit, it will be characterized by a diversity of opinion. In fact, one of the author's objectives in organizing this text is to chart a reasonable path through this diversity.

The NCR support for this effort has been tremendous. Don Piveral and Bill Henry have been unstinting in their management support, while the Data Pathing Systems Division salesmen have all participated with enthusiasm. In particular, Maureen Matthews' handling of office logistics, and Judi Cross with the word processor, made the whole project practical.

Contents

HANDBOOK OF
BAR CODING SYSTEMS

1. Introduction

During 1980, 1981, and well into 1982, bar-code technology progressed from a rather curious, obscure, more or less unused pattern on a few grocery items to an issue of major concern for every productive organization located anywhere. This was brought into sharp focus in 1982 by MIL-STD-1189, which requires a bar-code label on all items shipped to the U.S. Department of Defense—an order affecting as many as 50,000 companies acting as suppliers. Further, the auto industry has joined forces to require bar-code labels on every item moved between organizations in their environment—a decision involving at least 25,000 companies. Clearly, a very large number of industrial organizations must have a bar-code program if they expect to stay in business.

WHAT ARE BAR CODES?

A bar code is a printable machine language. In fact, bar codes are the only printable machine language which reproduces directly the bit-streams of ones and zeros which are the basis for the internal logic of all digital computers. While many different bar-code formats have been proposed, the only difference between one coding scheme and another is their byte formats: the way bits are organized into bytes. Bar codes are messages where information is encoded using the widths of printed bars, the widths of spaces between bars, and the relative positions of wide or narrow bars and spaces (i.e., unique wide or narrow combinations of black and white bars). They provide a means of creating labels which can be read by instruments.

While process control requires continuous attention, all other productive functions can be described in a series of discontinuous, discrete transactions. By placing a bar-code label on every significant item passing through each transaction of interest, bar coding makes it possible to automate the collection of transaction descriptions.

Bar coding is a memory form. Printing black bars on white paper is directly analogous to recording plus or minus bars in a magnetic medium. In fact, the basic formats used in these two technologies are identical. While information recorded in magnetic media can be packed at higher densities, and can be erased and rerecorded, printing bar codes on plain paper is much less expensive for many memory applications.

Bar coding is a network technique. Just as printed documents function as a basic means of communication between human minds, so bar-coded documents can link widely distributed instruments of diverse kinds into inexpensive communication networks.

Chapter 3 on "Label Technologies" and Chapter 4 on "Bar-Code Technology" discuss the broad issues of bar coding, while relevant details are covered in the Appendix.

WHY IS THERE A RUSH TO BAR CODES?

While the bar-code concept is not new, its early adoption was very slow to say the least. Originating attempts to use bar codes focused on two programs: point-of-sale transactions and rail car tracking. Each of these applications has been seriously burdened by the chicken/egg syndrome: there is not much point in installing expensive reading equipment until most items are labeled, and labeling serves no useful purpose unless labels are read.

However, at long last grocery businesses have reached the point of systems practicality. Even now some grocery stores attribute a savings of more than $1\frac{1}{2}\%$ of gross to the use of bar codes. Considering their normal profit margin, this manna from heaven is significant indeed. While only a few stores have yet to install readers, the program must already be considered a success. Ultimately bar-code reading will dominate point-of-sale applications. On the other hand, the rail tracking program has gone nowhere. Only a few cars have been labeled, and a meaningful number of reading stations has never been installed.

In the meantime, other similar programs have progressed to the point of viability: libraries, blood banks, etc. But the main impetus has come from Production Control or Management Information Systems (MIS) departments in organizations spread all across the discrete manufacturing community: meat processing, electronics, automotive, and others. By late 1981 almost every one interested in production control realized that its effectiveness was nowhere near what it could be. Here, most dramatically, was a tremendous opportunity for savings. Here are potential applications which exceed in scope the sum of the Defense Department and auto industry inventory control programs.

Various vendors rushed to respond to this opportunity with machine-readable labels based on OCR, magnetic-stripe, and bar-code technologies. Unfortunately, OCR and magnetic stripes perform some tasks very well; as a consequence it was not immediately apparent that they were dead-end prop- ositions as far as general production control tasks are concerned. Now it is recognized that bar coding is the only general-purpose printable machine language. Chapter 8 on "OCR Technology" and Chapter 9 on "Magnetic- Stripe Technology" detail the reasons for this conclusion.

WHAT SHOULD ONE KNOW ABOUT BAR CODES?

Bar coding involves four completely independent but interrelated processes: printing; reading; transforming from the space phase (what is printed) to a time phase, followed by an algorithm to decode the time phase; and a coding scheme which facilitates all the other processes. Existing commercial devices introduce major variables into each of these processes. As a result, the per- formance of current bar-code systems is diverse, and it is difficult to com- pare the specifications claimed for one system with those of some other.

Organizations hoping to bring standards to this disorder have not helped much. So far, the sum of their efforts has tended to add to the confusion, raise operating costs, and limit system performance. All this stems from the fact that those bar-code features which determine both print and read reliability are not well understood.

Chapter 6 on "Read Technology" and Chapter 7 on "Print Technology" provide a broad-brush perspective of this subject, with more detail in Appendix A, "Bar-Code System Issues." Appendix B, "Bar-Coding Schemes," lists the specific characteristics of a number of prominent bar codes.

WHO SHOULD KNOW ABOUT BAR CODES?

This text was organized specifically for those who are interested in maximiz- ing the efficiency of production control. These are represented primarily by the Production Control and Management Information Systems departmen- tal staffs of every member of the discrete manufacturing community—elec- tronics, automotive, aerospace, garment, food, and so on. Sooner or later all these organizations will be forced to establish a bar-code-supported pro- duction control system. There is no economically competitive alternative.

DEMANDS OF PRODUCTION CONTROL

The demand for improvement in production control efficiency stimulated the rapid adoption of the bar-code technology, once its potential was recognized. At the same time, the objectives of production control exercise all the facets of the bar-code art. Here the tasks of both reading and printing of bar codes in a wide variety of stituations must be addressed.

In contrast, markets concerned with point-of-sale transactions need only read bar codes. The labels which they read have been printed to one set of fairly rigid specifications. All their labels are batch-printed for them by other organizations. These labels are a part of the art work printed on the package containing the products to be sold. Those involved in point of sale do not even need to own a printer.

Libraries are better off than supermarkets because their labels are completely uniform, batch-printed in very high quality. Even medical laboratories, where labels are printed on demand from information held in a computer's archive memory, have few problems. Documents so printed are more or less uniform in quality and rigidly restricted in size and format.

On the other hand, production control draws on the flexibility offered by many different kinds of printers to create documents of any size, and in any configuration, which are appropriate for a variety of special purposes. These include the documents used to drive the work on the floor as well as labels for item identification.

A typical production control bar-code system is represented by an extensive facility where documents are printed on a wide variety of different kinds of printers in different coding densities, and where these documents are read by fixed-point laser scanners and hand-held laser scanners, and—at hundreds of different locations—by hand-held wands in various states of wear and manipulated by operators representing a broad range of understanding. Chapter 6 on "Read Technology" and Chapter 7 on "Print Technology" discuss the issues derived from this diversity. Here it can be seen that the availability of dot-matrix page-printers with a full graphics capability has been a key factor in developing the bar-code technology for production control purposes.

Because the full spectrum of bar-code issues is brought to focus by production control requirements, the objectives of production control are the underlying theme—the backbone, if you will—used to support and illustrate the application potential of the bar-code technology. Chapter 2 on "Objectives" discusses the reasons why production control has contributed so much to the momentum of adopting the bar-code technology, while Chapter 5 on "Documents" offers specific examples of bar-code tasks.

2. Objectives

I keep six honest serving men
(They taught me all I knew);
Their names are WHAT and WHY
and WHEN
And HOW and WHERE and WHO.
R. Kipling

In Kipling's little jingle lies the substance of effective manufacturing data-base management systems. In fact the actions taken, after definitive information is absorbed, is what management is all about. In general manufacturing circumstances, items (WHAT) move through a series of process steps wherein operators (WHO) located at work stations (WHERE) perform functions according to instructions (HOW) at specific times (WHEN). A series of transactions—acts, incidents, occurrences, and the like, both describe this flow and provide the means for its control. Automating the process of determining WHERE WHAT is WHEN—a transaction—allows continual computer analysis of WHY in order to advise WHO HOW established objectives can best be achieved (see Fig. 2.1).

In sophisticated systems these six functions (honest serving men all) are automated to the maximum degree. With automation, transaction descriptions are fed to computer memory as fast as they are generated. Once in memory, appropriate computations can proceed automatically and relevant information can be retrieved at any time in the form of analog plot, voice communication, electronic display, or printed page.

The effective management of manufacturing processes in general is based on continuous monitoring of captial utilization, inventory balance, staff activities, and the like, as these functions are evaluated against both new order and shipment forecasts. Achieving a general human understanding of the various factors affecting these processes will maximize managerial control

TRANSACTION

- WHAT
- WHERE
- WHEN

- HOW
- WHO

Figure 2.1.

over whatever transpires. In this context, computers perform the necessary analytical/documentary tasks faster, more reliably, and at lower cost than manual means.

In manufacturing processes, both products and associated documents flow through structured environments wherein productivity is described in terms of a series of predefined events (or transactions) which occur at specified system nodes. (A node is either a location or a time where a transaction takes place.) As a consequence, manufacturing data-base management systems are transaction-oriented. In fact, an entire manufacturing process can be defined when each transaction of importance is fully described. Here, the fact of a transaction communicated to a computer is specified in terms of its component parts: WHAT happened?, to WHAT did it happen?, WHERE did it happen?, WHEN did it happen?, and WHO made it happen? The terms "management" and "transaction control" are essentially synonymous as they relate to this subject. Definitive transaction descriptions are the key to managerial control, and the means by which computers obtain the descriptions of those items passing through each transaction set one facet of management's tone.

In one common practice, humans examine each passing item, then communicate their observations to computers via manually operated keyboards; skilled typists can enter messages at a rate of four to six characters per second. As an alternative, where each item is made identifiable by a machine-readable label, that label is read automatically at each system node, key entry is bypassed, and computers receive more accurate information in less time and at lower cost.

With bar-code labels relatively unskilled individuals, using hand held bar-code wands, can achieve a data entry rate of at least 20 characters per second with one fluid movement of the hand. Even this high speed can be significantly exceeded when hand movement is replaced by automatically swept light beams. But perhaps of more importance than speed is accuracy:

human carelessness, forgetfulness, and laziness cause errors which can never be eliminated by any manual means. (While voice entry can be substituted for key entry, this too is a human process and as such is as subject to human foibles as is key entry.)

Therefore an automated item-identification scheme is the basis for maximizing the effectiveness of manufacturing data-base management systems. When all items passing through a manufacturing transaction are appropriately labeled with label reading automated, the means for accomplishing precise audit traces are provided, while productivity is maximized in terms of movement control, throughput, security, and labor cost.

DRIVING FORCES

Major elements of the discrete manufacturing community have become dissatisfied with the effectiveness of their production control and are attempting significant changes in their modus operandi. These changes are noted in Figure 2.2.

MATERIAL RESOURCE PLANNING

- INCREASE IN DOCUMENT SOPHISTICATION
- INFORMATION COLLECTION AT WORK-STATIONS
- KEY-ENTRY BYPASS
- DISTRIBUTED INTELLIGENCE

Figure 2.2.

While a number of factors impinge on this pervasive movement, a major driving force is the concept of material resource planning, or MRP.

MRP is perhaps a misunderstood subject full of bias and emotion. What is really meant by this phrase? To introduce some precision to this subject and eliminate confusion to the degree possible, this definition is suggested as at least sufficing here: MRP is the computer-aided art of causing a selected item to arrive at a designated location within a very narrow time frame. Here the operative term is "selected item." If the selected item's transit is to be computer-directed, as it will be in any complex situation, that item must be identified by some automated means: that is, it must be possible to identify that item by a machine-readable label. Therefore any truly successful MRP program is based on some technique for machine-readable labeling. MRP aside, it should be obvious that you can do a better job if you know where everything is, and this most assuredly requires machine-readable labels!

The subject does not end here by any means, however, for MRP is merely the icing on the cake: beneath this icing are a number of other considerations where machine-readable labeling is an imperative. Consider, for instance, the subject of tool calibration control. Tool crib logistics in general are well exercised in every organization. Were the right tools issued for the job? Who is now responsible for these tools? Was a complete set of tools issued? Where are these tools? And later: were all the tools returned? Obviously, bar coding minimizes the effort required in answering these questions. Here each tool can be rationalized against a predetermined kit list and the tools checked against both an authorization and an ID card, all covered by appropriate bar-coded labels.

But the problem goes well beyond tool location control to tool condition control. For example, in the aircraft industry, every set of wire strippers used must be maintained in a particular state of calibration. At the very least, each set of wire strippers must be retrieved from the factory floor at the end of some period where time-in-use alone is grounds for suspecting their condition. This means that every set of wire strippers must have its own unique record identified by its own serial number.

In another example, the field service of complex equipment is always a particularly poignant problem. Further, the experience of the field service organization impinges directly on the effectiveness of quality assurance. At least one organization has tightened its field operations around a replacement policy to the degree this is possible, implementing the order, "Find the defective part, replace it, and get out!" Each field service engineer is issued a portable terminal which can be driven by a bar-code wand, and every part is serialized. As the engineer replaces a part, he wands the label on the old part, then the label on the new part, and goes on his way. At the end of the day he dumps the contents of his portable terminal back to the home plant over a telephone line. The next morning this information is delivered to Inventory Control, the maintenance supervisor, and Quality Assurance. By these means all records are kept current, the maintenance supervisor knows what his people are doing, and Quality Assurance operates with the definitive index of their success.

As long as a part has to have a serial number for the above purposes, it might just as well be placed as early as possible and used by Production Control during the manufacturing processes. In one example, bar-code labels are attached to printed circuit boards prior to board exposure to a vacuum bake cycle. This vacuum bake process, in addition to thoroughly drying the boards, has the effect of pulling the label tight down against the board and curing the smear resistant bar-code printing ink. The result is a very durable label able to withstand the heat of the flow solder process and subsequent cleaning operations in both aqueous and freon-based solutions. This label can be beam-scanned at each work station during manufacturing processes and then wand-scanned for inventorying, shipping, and field service functions.

DOCUMENT SOPHISTICATION

The class of documents discussed here do not include postoperational reports. Rather, the documents of interest are those used by Production Control to drive the work on the factory floor—the documents used to communicate Production Control's intent to operators in work stations. These are "operational" documents.

An increase in document sophistication (see Fig. 2.3) is a basic objective. This implies some kind of improvement over the way Production Control communicates now. These communications include detailing the means by which operators are required to report progress. While every organization has not by any means been using the same technique, a punched card is the nearest thing to a past common denominator. Such a card provides space for 80 machine-readables and 80 human-readables presented in a very rigid format. The 80 human-readables are used to reference other documents, while the 80 machine-readables are used to automate the collection of only one

INCREASE IN DOCUMENT SOPHISTICATION

- ON-LINE CREATION OF OPERATIONAL DOCUMENTS

- INCREASE IN QUANTITY AND FLEXIBILITY OF HUMAN READABLES

- INCREASE IN QUANTITY AND FLEXIBILITY OF MACHINE READABLES

Figure 2.3.

part of a transaction description. The other parts must be supplied by other means—a manually operated keyboard.

A major problem associated with punched cards is the cost of the hardware required to both punch and read the punched information. The cost of a card punch is such that it cannot be supported by the activities of a typical work center, while a card reader is many dollars out of the question for a work station. As a direct consequence, the operators performing in a system based on punched cards must spend a great deal of time wandering around to get their cards read and trying to figure out what documents are referenced.

Derived directly from the above discussion, an increase in document sophistication means something more effective, and less expensive to use, than a punched card. An improved document must provide space for more machine-readables, and more human-readables with the flexibility to print both in any configuration desired. In addition, the reader for the machine-readables must be of a cost low enough to allow their use in work stations, while the cost of a printer should, at the very least, be low enough for work centers. Here flexibility includes flexibility of print/read hardware location as well as flexibility of format. The bar-code technology has the potential of fulfilling all these objectives.

PERSONAL TERMINAL

When computer technology was first applied to production control problems, the computers themselves were located in some central bastion to and from which documents flowed in a not very efficient or timely stream. Only specialists were allowed to communicate directly with a computer, and their lingua franca was the perforated card. Then, with the advent of distributed data processing, on-line terminals were located in work centers, where the operators who actually performed work could communicate directly with a computer. In these circumstances one work-center terminal supports the activities of several dozen work stations.

There is now a strong movement to migrate the data-collection points from work centers to work stations. If this is done, efficiency is improved (so the logic goes) because an operator does not have to leave the work station to communicate with a computer. However, a successful response to this migratory pressure must address a number of issues, not the least of which is cost. If it can be assumed that today a work-center terminal, serving 36 work stations, costs $3,600, this can be distributed in the amount of $100 at the work-station level. But if efficiency is improved, perhaps there is something more than $100 to spend for a personal (work-station) terminal.

On a more technical plane, the mere fact that terminals are located in work centers imposes a limit to the rate of communication demanded of the data path linking terminals with a computer. As only one operator can use a terminal at a time, a physical queue limits computer access. At the present time, the performance of many systems is limited by the peak traffic on their data path. It would not be possible for these to absorb the order of magnitude increase in traffic implied by migration to work stations. With terminals in work stations, some electronic means is needed to counterpart the physical clustering functions which results automatically from the use of work-center terminals. Then, too, personal terminals need buffer memories to hold messages for the short period required for an electronic queue to exercise its choice. Here the buffer supports the equivalent of the in-hand and in-mind information which is otherwise held by an operator while waiting to use a terminal. (See Fig. 2.4.)

Not only does a work-center terminal provide clustering for the work stations it serves, it also communicates the status of its availability by the number of operators waiting in queue to go on-line. That is, an operator wishing to use a terminal can look and, if there is someone already on-line, he knows he must wait until he is through. Or, if there are two people in queue, he can become number three if he so chooses. A personal terminal must provide this same information by some means or other. A red light, indicating that a system is busy, is hardly a satisfactory answer.

As the migration from work center to work stations gathers momentum, it becomes increasingly apparent that a bar-code wand is all the personal terminal needs in many work stations. At least, this is true if the wand features a small buffer memory and a simple tutorial display (see Fig. 2.5).

KEY BYPASS

Keyboards are expensive and vulnerable to harsh environments. Their long-term reliability is questionable, while their use is both time-consuming and prone to human error. Bar coding offers an alternative to keyboards, as a

INFORMATION COLLECTION AT
WORK-STATIONS

- INEXPENSIVE PERSONAL TERMINALS

- CLUSTERING

- ELECTRONIC QUEUING

Figure 2.4.

PERSONAL TERMINAL

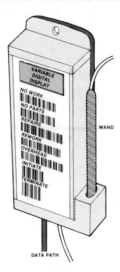

Figure 2.5.

means of data entry at the local level which is faster, less erratic, and significantly less expensive (see Fig. 2.6). In many applications, this adds up to better performance at lower cost.

However, bar coding (or other machine-readable labeling technology) is not the only means of key bypass—of entering information without exercising a keyboard. Hardwiring to sensors, sampling phenomena of interest, has a tradition which is at least as long as that of a keyboard. Direct connections are also, then, a means of key bypass.

This is a significant thought, because the movement of data collection points from work centers to work stations places the data-collecting hardware in close proximity to the processes being reported upon. In other

KEY-ENTRY BYPASS

- MACHINE-READABLE LABELS

- INTERFACING

- ACTIVITY MONITORING

Figure 2.6.

words, it is possible to perform certain functions in work stations which were not possible in work centers. Why not hardwire and be done with it? Why not count pieces directly? Why not peek into a process-control loop to see what is going on? While the answers to these questions will be positive in many circumstances, there are factors which must be considered.

First is the issue of economics achieved through standardization. Where a human operates a terminal (or performs any other function, for that matter), that human can be regarded as offering a standard of sorts. A terminal need only be designed to optimize its relations with a human to expect reasonable standard product sales. In other words, the activities which take place in work centers are standardized to serve many functions by the human interface between terminal and function. On the other hand, the activities of one work station must be presumed to be different from those of every other work station. Any attempts to connect a general-purpose data-processing system to the equipment in a work station by hardwire requires a custom interface. While it is theoretically possible to supply this, the economics are a problem.

Second, can the instruments in a work station supply information of interest? In many circumstances the answer to this question is "no." Consider, for instance, a process controller, either loop or sequence. As many of these instruments are now designed, all they can provide is a knowledge of their status, which is of small use to Production Control. They simply do not retain a record of their performance in a form subject to query. However, the presence of an accumulator of some sort, such as in piece counting, is another matter. Here, the interface is electronically simple and the information supplied is of legitimate value.

Third is the problem of communications. Is there some practical means of tapping into the data paths of a wide variety of systems—numeric control, energy balance, QC test setups, process control, and the like, including various instruments which may be involved in particular transactions? Is there a means of common interface? The purpose of any interface technique is to provide an effective communication link over which messages are carried in a nonambiguous way, among a group of interconnected devices. Communication objectives in this sense strive for "universality"—the ability for one device to communicate with any other device over a standard communication system. Unfortunately, there is no such standard. Each type of device inherently prefers to communicate in a particular fashion, and there are many such fashions. Therefore, making any particular device operate over a standard interface of any kind is likely to increase its complexity, hence its cost, and may well constrict its potential performance in terms of speed and flexibility.

Fourth, one may ask: as long as there is two-way communication between

Production Control and work-station processes, can this communication link be used to control these processes? In general, this is not possible. The basic rhythms of systems optimized for data collection and of those optimized for process control are different and definitely at odds. Process control requires a system dedicated to one purpose with a loop reliability and a response time directed by that purpose. Process-control systems are driven by the process they control and must include an imperative of response (the "look at me" demand). In contrast, production control systems follow the dictates of a centralized authority which in no way can be kept informed of the immediate needs of one process sharing a system with many other processes.

DISTRIBUTED INTELLIGENCE

No matter what their application, extensive computer systems have generally been organized around the premise that memory and processing power must be centralized because they are very expensive. As a result, many factory data-collection systems utilize a central processor which serves a number of terminals. This service both supplies memory and processing power to each terminal whenever required to complete a transaction, and acts as a buffer between transaction-oriented terminals and extensive archived memories housed in batch-oriented number crunchers.

In some systems a central processor polls every terminal within a time interval which is short enough (perhaps a half second) to be sure any particular terminal receives the support it requires when it is required. Here the cost of a processor can be justified only when it supports a fairly large number of terminals. With a processor acting as a dominant cost factor, it is not economical to initiate a program with a few terminals. With constant polling, and terminal responses, the heavy traffic on the data path is a system performance limitation.

As the prices for memory and processing power drop, these functions tend to move from central locations out into the terminals at a system's periphery. Once a terminal has its own memory and the associated processing power, it may no longer require the services of a central processor. Not only does it perform the tasks assigned on its own volition, but it can act as its own buffer between batch-oriented and transaction-oriented functions.

Following this concept, it can make sense to build a system one terminal at a time. Here the system philosophy changes from one where there is constant, frantic communication with every terminal over a hardwired data path, to one where each terminal is told what is expected of it at the beginning of an accounting period and is queried as to its performance at the end of that period. While a terminal is performing its assigned tasks during an account period, there is no traffic on the data path. A terminal receives its instructions at any time prior to the beginning of an account period, and is polled for performance after completion of work, or at any time during that account period, if so desired (see Fig. 2.7).

With a quiet data path during account periods, any terminal can ask for new instructions if its performance is aberrant—that is, if for any reason the tasks assigned cannot be performed. In fact, in many circumstances access to a hardwired data path is not used during account periods; a terminal needs such access only while receiving instructions or responding. Since hardwired data paths are a significant expense in factory data collection systems and impose constraints of sorts as to the location of terminals, a system based on account period performance is less expensive to install and infinitely more flexible in terms of terminal-location possibilities.

The fact that a terminal does not need to be connected to a system during an account period leads to the portable terminal concept (see Fig. 2.8). As bar coding provides a means, as an alternative to keyboards, for communicating with computer systems at the local level, a combination of bar-code wands and account-period terminals results in simple, rugged, extremely flexible products particularly appropriate for factory applications. The synergistic possibilities resulting from the combination of portable terminals with the bar code technology are of major interest to those who wish to restructure production control.

IDENTIFICATION

Hungry citizens, contemplating soup purchased by the can, focus their attention on type, quantity, manufacturer, and of course price. As far as projected purchases are concerned, information of interest is commonly supplied by the detailed product description, application notes, and other sales

DISTRIBUTED INTELLIGENCE

- ACCOUNT PERIOD INSTRUCTIONS
- ACCOUNT PERIOD POLLING
- ABERRATION RESPONSE
- OFF-LINE INTERACTIONS

Figure 2.7.

Figure 2.8. A portable terminal. Reproduced with permission of MSI Data Corporation.

material appearing on a can's label (see Fig. 2.9). Every can of soup meeting the same type/quantity/manufacturer criteria is assumed to be exactly the same as every other can.

Customers are not directly interested in computer entry problems when in a soup-buying mood. However, they may well be concerned with the time spent waiting in a checkout line and, because of this concern, might wish to see this waiting time reduced by an automated item-identification system. And the manager of an establishment selling canned soup is interested in the same issues as are his customers, but for additional reasons. He wishes to precisely identify and record whatever takes place in each point-of-sale, shelf-stocking, warehouse-inventorying, ordering, and receiving transaction. He is doubtless very eager to introduce relevant information to a computer by automating entry processes to the maximum degree possible.

LABEL REQUIREMENTS

- PRODUCT   • LOCATION
- PACKAGE   • HUMAN
- DOCUMENT

Figure 2.9.

The Universal Product Code (UPC) and the European Article Numbering Code (EAN) were developed as a means of expediting computer entry transactions for situations similar to those described above. One version of the UPC defines a bar-code message having two fields of five digits each. One field is a numeric rendition of the manufacturer, while the second field numerically indicates that particular manufacturer's unique product—its type and size. Neither field is capable of supplying further information for any other purpose.

The UPC serves the above processes very well as long as they are routine. But the system breaks down and is of no help in directing an investigation, if the contents of one can are found variant. Back-checking a soup problem involves a laborious manual review of ordering and receiving documents in an attempt to identify the manufacturer's batch to which the can of interest belongs. As soup cans commonly have no unique identification which discriminates between like cans, identifying a deviant batch—and from this determining the reason for the deviation—may well be impossible.

While serialization of soup cans is probably not worthwhile, serial numbers are commonly found on products with higher intrinsic values. Certainly serial numbers can be used to precisely identify almost any unique item. However, both UPC-type codes and serial numbers have one common limiting characteristic: each addresses only a unique location in a look-up table and is useful only when accessing such a table. Reliance on look-up tables imposes severe restrictions on systems operating in dynamic off-line or human interface modes. As many manufacturing-type transactions could not be carried out if they had to depend on look-up tables, something more is required of a labeling technique.

3. Label Technologies

Responding to the WHAT requirement, all items involved in manufacturing transactions must be capable of both human and machine recognition. These items include products, documents, and containers. The question WHERE adds a variety of location possibilities. Each can be identified by an appropriately coded label.

It must then be possible to utilize various automated means of applying coded information to a wide variety of media capable of withstanding rugged manufacturing environments. For documents this includes tags, cards, tickets, labels, preprinted forms, typing paper, and even metal strips. Relevant containers run the gamut from boxes and cartons through trays, bins, jars, and envelopes. Coded labels of various kinds can be formed as integral parts of products, either by affixation or by casting, etching, grinding, cutting, impacting, or other fabricating techniques.

Further, it should be possible to reproduce labeled documents in multiple copies by offset, letter press, photo composition, flexographic, lithography/offset, xerographic, or other printing or copying methods. Nor should message-coding technologies be restrictive. Message lengths should be optional and all alphabetic as well as numeric ciphers should be available. (There is no rational reason for an alphanumeric designator system already in use to be changed, just because automation is added.)

Coded messages should provide the maximum of information in the minimum space. They should be readily reproducible on various media, and easy to understand and economical to read in any transaction. Transaction identification should be possible with interactive terminals, automated terminals, instrumented terminals, and portable terminals, using either hand-held wands or automated scanning devices of various kinds.

Flexibility is an important feature of any coding technique used in these applications. It should be possible to encipher almost any message which might otherwise be constructed from conventional human-readable characters. (Just because all alphanumeric characters are available does not mean that all must be used in all circumstances. MIL–STD–100A forbids the use of *I, O, Q,* and *X,* while *Z* and *S* might deserve elimination in some circumstances to avoid visual confusion with the numbers *2* and *5*.)

For maximizing human recognition, character chains in characteristic patterns are desirable. Dates should look like dates (i.e., 2/5/79), and dollar signs should accompany funds. (One of the first companies offering point-of-sale terminals went belly-up because of the format used in identifying transactions: the clerks continually confused prices with the number of items still left in stock!) By organizing characteristic character chains, it is possible to encourage humans (and even computers!) to recognize that a particular formatted character set refers to a particular type of item such as a part, purchase order, work order, or ID card. Here the symbols "–", "." and "/" are invaluable in establishing a wide variety of characteristic segmentations.

LABEL TYPES

There are three basic types of machine-readable labels now under consideration for discrete-manufacture applications (see Fig. 3.1): optical character recognition (OCR), magnetic stripe, and bar code. (Optical character recognition is the ability of an instrument to recognize or read human-readable characters.) While other labeling technologies such as MICR (magnetic ink character recognition) and embossment can be machine-read, there is now no interest in their adoption for the purposes at hand.

Of the three types listed, magnetic stripe and OCR are definitely restricted in their capabilities; only bar coding can be used as a generally applied labeling technique. OCR can be eliminated simply because its read reliability is

TYPES OF LABELS

- OPTICAL CHARACTER RECOGNITION (OCR)

- MAGNETIC STRIPE

- BAR CODE
  - CODE-39
  - UPC
  - EAN
  - CODABAR
  - 2/5

Figure 3.1.

not adequate for this application. According to the published literature, the substitution error rate is 1/10,000 for a restricted character set. This in itself is so bad that a full character set is seldom attempted.

As an expression of faith in technological progress, it might be assumed that someday low-cost OCR reading will be accomplished with a low substitution error rate for a full character set. However, such faith is clearly misplaced, for with OCR each character must be scanned many times in order to search out those differences which distinguish one character from another. (For instance, what is the real difference, as determined by scan, between an *O*, a *C*, a *D*, and a *0*?) This multiscan requirement makes OCR reading significantly slower and significantly more expensive than bar-code scanning—theoretically, as well as practically. In this respect, OCR has "heroic" implications, while bar coding is "elegant." That is, if enough money is spent for a reading system, anything—including OCR—is possible. But where cost is a consideration, bar coding offers the clear answer.

The technology which brings this situation into focus is the recent availability of mechanical dot-matrix printers with a "full graphics" capability. These function on-line as general-purpose printing terminals and can be used to place bar-coded messages on any document in any configuration. Unfortunately, most of the mechanical dot-matrix printers now on the market will not print quality bar-code labels, because the mechanical tolerances to which they are constructed do not allow the necessary precision of dot placement. There are a few machines which will do the job, but even these are limited to a maximum cipher density set by their mechanical tolerances.

Further, it should be noted that while certain mechanical printers currently available can be made to work, their performance leaves much to be desired. Their inherent characteristic of variation, in both print contrast and dimension, is barely tolerable. On the other hand, various electrostatic printers produce high-quality documents. While the laser electrostatic machines tend to be high-priced, less expensive devices utilizing the electrostatic technology should be on the market shortly.

CODE CLASSIFICATION

Label coding can be expanded to serve additional functions designed to minimize the need for access to look-up tables. Item-identification schemes can be developed to carry messages which have off-line implications and which can be interpreted precisely by humans in human-interface modes. This is accomplished by applying various classification indices to coding systems.

Because classification is potentially awkward in terms of message length and complexity, there is an extensive body of argument against its use in labeling systems. Obviously, these arguments won out in the choices which led to the formulation of the UPC. However, classification is a necessary attribute of any data base, and the issue is solely one of whether classification should appear in the label or only be applied to look-up information held in a computer's memory.

The answer to the argument of "label classification versus no classification" lies in an analysis of the functions to be performed during each transaction. That is, any functions which are better performed off-line must be supported by information which can be established off-line. If item identity enters into an off-line transaction, whatever classification is required to support that transaction must appear as a part of that item in some form or other. Sorting is one example of an automated task which can be performed off-line, if the information against which the sort is decided is available either in a label or as a characteristic of the sorted item.

Classification is accomplished by recognizing some commonality that has transaction control significance. In other words, a code can be classified in such a way that the classification will direct transactions of interest. (This is sometimes called SEUGO or "significant end use goal orientation.") Such transaction direction can accomplish a variety of purposes. For instance, Shipping is interested in destinations (customers), while Receiving's concern is with sources (vendors), and project managers dream of stratification (levels), while production managers search out common manufacturing processes. Salesmen love snappy acronyms designed to lodge in customers' minds, while stockrooms are best organized around product functions. The search for commonality can be endless. Organizing custom classification systems is expensive and fraught with data-base conflict possibilities. Professor Inyong Ham is reputed to have identified 77 "standard" classification systems already in the public domain. (The Russians may have developed one of the more sophisticated systems in this respect.)

Complicated or not, classification is used to direct off-line transactions and is definitely required in many circumstances. It is used to convert a file into a data base, and that data base can be distributed out onto the production floor via labeling to the degree of its potential utility in that context.

TERMINOLOGY

The terms "character," "cipher," "message," "code," and "label," as commonly found in the literature, have different meanings when used by different authors, which leads to some confusion. In this discussion, *character* refers both to the human recognizable roman rendition of the alphabet and to the conventional arabic numbers. A *cipher* is a coded character designed for maximum ease of reading by electronic means, while a *message* is a string of either characters or ciphers which imparts information either to humans or directly to computers. A *header,* commonly used to identify the information carried by a document, is either an *abstract* or a coded label.

The word *label* refers to a descriptive message applied to an item by any means, for purposes of identification. A label in this sense can either be printed directly onto a document or be engraved into the material from which a product is fabricated. (In some forums the word "label" refers only to a strip of material which is attached to an item by adhesion. This is in contrast to a *tag,* which is attached by some means other than adhesion. Here, both tags and labels are considered to be *tickets.*)

A *code* is a system of symbols arbitrarily assigned either to conventional characters or to messages for purposes of either clarification or obfuscation. A character can be coded with a cipher, while a message can be coded with either groups of characters or groups of ciphers.

HUMAN INTERFACE

Throughout many otherwise automated flow processes, there are circumstances where a human might just as well exercise his own judgment independent of instrumentation or computer advice. As one example, the contents of the boxes found in King Tut's tomb did not match the labels, but the same wrong contents were always associated with the same labels. Apparently, the gentlemen filling these funeral containers recognized the principle of commonality but could not determine the significance of this commonality, because they could not read the labels.

While the example is archaeological, the problem is contemporary. The annoyance of Tut's "Ba," when finding beans in a can labeled "peaches," is a graphic but not unfamiliar experience of production managers. This was not the last time, by any means, when the will of the gods (management) was frustrated because the priests (MIS practitioners) failed to bring the fellaheen into the act.

In any economically conceived automated system, all transactions do not carry the same weight in every analytical process. All transactions do not necessarily involve computer interaction and may not require complete descriptions. For instance, consider the process of rationalization in the cases of tool with product, contents with package, document with product, and bills with receipts: in each instance, are the two parts related? Some of these functions are best performed off-line without the help or even the knowledge of a computer. While the fact of such an occurrence may well be vital to the flow process, the time or location of the action has no particular managerial significance, and there is nothing much to be gained by carrying such event descriptions in computerized data bases. But at the same time all items involved in off-line activities of this sort must be fully identified, or the intended transaction might not be consummated.

LABEL CHARACTERISTICS

Attempts to quantify the performance of machine-readable labeling systems often reference three fundamental characteristics (see Fig. 3.2):

LABEL CHARACTERISTICS

- **FIRST READ RATE**

- **SUBSTITUTION ERROR RATE**

- **PRINT CONTRAST RATIO**
  — SIGNAL STRENGTH

Figure 3.2.

The *first read rate* measures the chance of getting a read with the first scan. If on the average, for instance, it takes two attempts to get a read, the FRR is said to be 50%. Of course, it would be nice if a reading was obtained with every attempt. Unfortunately, for a variety of reasons 100% read-success is not possible.

FRR relates primarily to systems where labels are to be read with hand-held wands. Where a bar-coded label is scanned with a laser beam, which repeats its scan hundreds of times each second, the FRR has little significance. In addition, where the same information is repeated within one message, as is common practice with the magnetic stripe technology, the meaning of FRR becomes somewhat obscure.

On the surface, the FRR appears to be just a "convenience" factor. A low rate is doubtless annoying, but certainly not "traumatic." Not being able to read a message at all is a bit worse, because the only recourse is key entry. But at least key entry is possible. However, this possibility can be a trap, for a high FRR is a requirement if human confidence in a system is to be upheld. Experience shows that, where possible, humans tend to abandon hand-held wand-reading systems with a low FRR in favor of the old, familiar keyboard.

If there is anything worse than a low FRR, including even a "no read," it is a "wrong read." Reading information incorrectly is catastrophic. The presence of incorrect information in a data base represents an endless source of confusion and expense.

The *substitution error rate* defines those conditions where a reading provides the wrong information and the fact of a bad read is not immediately apparent. The SER is a measure of how many times a wrong read can be expected. This is an extremely important criterion, as it impinges directly on the quality of data-base integrity. SERs apply both to hand-held wand scans and to fully automated means of reading.

In many read systems, high FRRs and low SERs tend to be opposing objectives. The FRR is a highly visible factor, showing up in every attempt to read, while the SER lurks in the boskage more or less unobserved. A false read is usually discovered well after the fact.

The *print contrast ratio* is an indication of signal strength—the amount of information available from which a reading can be composed. With the bar-code and OCR technologies, PCR is the difference in light reflectivity between printed marks and the backgrounds against which those marks are printed. Magnetic stripes have an equivalent PCR in the difference between two magnetic field strengths. PCRs have a definite effect on the signal/noise ratio present in the electrical signals resulting from a label read.

It is not possible to directly relate read success, in terms of FRR and SER, either to a label technology per se, or to the coding scheme used within a technology. Machine reading of labels addresses space context (what is printed), the translation of space to time (the generation of a coded voltage by the transform process), and the algorithm used to decode the voltage. The coding scheme used, the print quality achieved (dimensional precision as well as PCR), the algorithm applied, and the electronic support circuitry represent a complete system. The quantities FRR and SER can be applied only to the performance of a specific system.

In this respect, a system's overall performance is affected by the performance of every one of its component parts. Some coding schemes have the potential to outperform other schemes, while algorithms can be concocted to favor FRR at the expense of SER.

OCR/BAR-CODE COMBINATION

A combination of bar-code ciphers and human-readable characters (conventional alphanumeric graphic symbols) provides the only practical, economic means of accomplishing all label objectives. Although bar-code ciphers are not subject to human interpretation, they can be read with inexpensive instruments. On the other hand, while automated OCR is a relatively expensive process, humans easily interpret alphabetic and numeric characters. Since the process of reading bar codes is concerned only with the information contained in the reflectivity differences encountered over a single line drawn through a bar-coded message, bar coding is the most cost-effective means of labeling items for machine-reading purposes. That is, the electronic circuitry required is of minimum complexity.

As humans best read characters, and machines, bar codes, combining the two techniques provides the best of both worlds. Since the cost of printing either human characters, bar-code ciphers, or combinations of the two is now essentially the same (using dot-matrix printers), the decision to provide both maximizes flexibility without increasing cost. A logical format prints the human-readable equivalent directly above (or below) the cipher represented. Under these circumstances, the human-readable characters constitute an *echo line.*

While a combination of human-readable characters and machine-readable ciphers represents the best of both worlds, the issue here is bar coding. The next chapter gives a broad treatment to this subject, with a more detailed treatment provided by the appendices.

4. Bar-Code Technology

Bar codes offer a basic, documentary means of communication between computer systems. Here communication possibilities are two-way: it is possible for material printed by one system to be read and digested by any other system without recourse to human interpretation. In these circumstances, printed texts are read either manually by the stroke of a hand-held wand, or automatically by the sweep of a light beam or by electronic linear arrays.

The bar-coding art involves three separate, completely independent (but interrelated) technologies: (1) printing; (2) transforming from the space phase (as printed) to the time phase; and (3) applying an appropriate algorithm to decode the time phase.

A number of different bar-coding schemes have been developed over the years which are now available for general use. Each of these represents a different response to a spectrum of objectives where individual objectives within this spectrum are assigned different weights by each coding method. Code density, character set, print tolerance, read tolerance, and the like are all factors worthy of consideration. An appreciation of relevant objectives, and their influence on coding decisions, can be of assistance when evaluating the potential of a particular code: it is nice to know what a code designer had in mind when he organized his code.

Maximum first read rate and minimum substitution error rate are two basic objectives which can be applied to all bar codes. There are a number of possible safeguards which might be used in a coding system to assure a minimal substitution error rate: fixed-length bit-streams; a similar pattern of bars and spaces in each cipher (the same number, and in the same order); odd/even parity for the bar/space pattern in each cipher; the same number of bits in each cipher (each cipher should be the same physical length as is every other cipher); odd/even parity for the zeros/ones in each cipher; and a module (or block check) cipher in every message. If any of these factors is compromised or omitted, a substitution error rate results which is larger than it might otherwise be.

The cipher set, which is used to compose a given bar-code system, determines the number of decisions which must be made by a given algorithm at each attempt to read a cipher. The greater the number of decisions to be made, the higher the substitution error rate and the lower the first read rate. In a numeric-only cipher set, there are only ten possible decisions to be made for each attempt to read a given cipher. In an alphanumeric set, the number of decisions jumps to thirty-six. While a full ASCII system calls for 128 decisions, these might be reduced to the 64-character ½ ASCII set more commonly used.

In many reading systems each character of a bar-coded message is interpreted separately. In this sense, a *rejection rate* is a measure of individual character read success. The first read rate is, then, a function both of the cipher rejection rate and the number of ciphers in a message. If the rejection rate is 1%, as it may well be, then a message with 20 ciphers will have a first read rate of about 82 percent.

The number of coding components used in a coding system also impinges on the number of decisions which must be made by an algorithm. For instance, a code which uses four components (wide/narrow bars and wide/narrow spaces) experiences less strain in decoding than does one which uses eight coding components (bars and spaces each of which is one, two, three, or four elements wide), because it is easier to decide which of four than which of eight.

A decoding algorithm is organized against the assumption that the space-time transform will be accomplished at some constant velocity plus or minus some variation of that otherwise constant velocity. The longer a message in terms of physical length, the more difficult is the task of maintaining that velocity constant while hand-wanding. As a result, the longer the message beyond some practical length, the lower the first read rate, the higher the substitution error rate, and the slower the decoding process. Three inches might represent some practical maximum length for bar-coded messages which are to be read manually. This of course is a completely arbitrary suggestion, not applicable to beam scan but probably desirable for linear array. This need to minimize the physical length of a bar-code message leads to the objective of printing in the highest possible density. Assuming a requirement for START, STOP, and "modulo check" ciphers, messages printed on a Printronix have a maximum of seven ciphers; on an Intermec, 28; and on electrostatic printers, at least forty-two.

It is axiomatic that messages not printed within specifications are difficult to read. Therefore the poorer the print quality, the lower the first read rate and the higher the substitution error rate. Batch-printed labels using Flexography, Gravure, or Letterpress, such as those printed for point-of-sale purposes, can be printed to fairly close specifications. However, when attempts are made to print bar-coded messages picked at random from computer archives, many of the printers now in use do not print reliably to specifications. (Rather, the specifications for a bar-code system are written to accept what is printed with a particular printer. Tying specifications to the idiosyncrasies of a given printer compromises the performance of a code when used with other printers.) Not only is the print contrast ratio highly variable with many printers (particularly with mechanical dot-matrix printers), but the variable spaces between bars, which are a significant part of coding schemes, are commonly ignored. All this puts quite a burden on the decoding algorithms.

Now, of course, it is possible to design an algorithm which will read what is printed whether or not what is printed meets reasonable specifications. But this approach presumes the use of only one printer, or perhaps one type of printer, in a particular system—most certainly, a limiting presumption. The use of an algorithm to read non-reg printing can only result in lower read performance than otherwise possible. Some sloppy algorithms are now offered which are organized to give the highest possible first read rate under the worst conditions. Unfortunately, these function at the expense of the substitution error rate. With the first read rate's high visibility, and the substitution error rate's obscurity, these algorithms are based on the assumption that what you don't know won't hurt you!

COMPOSITION

Bar-code ciphers are constructed from a series of dark and light bars organized, according to specific rules, into various patterns which represent letters, numerals, and other familiar human-readable symbols. Here the dark bars are what is printed, while the light bars are the spaces between each pair of dark bars. A complete bar-coded message is represented by a "picket fence" of dark bars wherein the number of dark bars, the relative positions of these dark bars within the fence, their variable widths, the variable widths of the accompanying light bars (spaces), and the relative positions of the light bars carry the coded information. Bar coding offers these five possible variables for coding purposes.

A bar-coded message is composed of some number of bar-coded ciphers. While it is possible to break the picket fence down into its component parts, or ciphers, this must be done electronically, since it is very difficult to pick out individual ciphers from a complete text by visual means, when the fence looks more or less continuous to the human eye.

The structural rules around which bar patterns are organized address two basic objectives. In one, a given bar pattern is identified as being a legitimate member of a specific cipher set. In the other, a bar pattern is identified as being a particular, unique member of that set. In some respects, these two objectives are in opposition, for the greater the number of coding features which establish commonality among a family of ciphers, the better, while the greater the number of features which establish cipher uniqueness, the better. From this apparent conflict it may be deduced that the greater the number of code features available to be distributed between these two objectives, the higher the quality of coding technique.

Bar codes are a machine language designed specifically to introduce information to digital computers. To accomplish this objective with dispatch, bar-code formats should be consistent with computer language. The machine languages of digital computers are binary in form, with all information composed as a series of ones and zeros. If bar codes are to be most effective in their avowed purpose, they too should be composed of ones and zeros.

Within the vitals of digital computers, the presence of a one is related to a clock pulse. (The "clock" of a digital computer consists of a series of pulses which are used to divide time into equal increments.) Here, if a clock pulse occurs in one channel, and at the same time a matching pulse occurs in some other channel, that matching pulse is said to indicate a one. On the other hand, if there is no matching pulse in the second channel at the time of clock-pulse occurrence, the absence of such a pulse indicates a zero. By relating all information to a clock-track in this fashion, it is possible to separate out the presence of individual zeros as these occur in groups of sequential zeros. That is, by the use of a clock track, it is possible to tell a string of zeros from an otherwise quiet channel.

Duplicating the above philosophy directly, it is quite possible to print bar codes in two (or more) tracks where the space phase, inherent to bar codes, reproduces the time phase of a computer (see Fig. A.1). Here one track is used as the clock track while another track carries the bit-stream, an appropriate series of ones and zeros. (The TEKSCAN code of Appendix B is one form of clocked code.) While such a coding scheme takes up a lot of space, its main disadvantage lies in the requirement of reading two tracks simultaneously. That is, it is relatively expensive to read, since it costs more to read two channels than one.

Schedule A.2, Item 1, in Appendix A combines a clock track with an information track. This is done by using the leading edge of each bar as the clock. As long as these leading edges occur at a more or less constant clock rate, the width of a bar can be used to indicate either a one or a zero. That is, a narrow bar can be used for a zero, and a wide bar for a one. While this coding technique has the merit of consuming only one channel, it is otherwise wasteful of space. For it actually requires both a bar and a space to indicate either a one (wide bar, narrow space) or a zero (narrow bar, wide space).

Numerous so-called "self-clocking" codes have been formulated. These make it possible to reconstruct the clock during the reading process. Most of these address the issue of how to get the most information into the least possible space.

Bar codes are printed. This means that bar-coding schemes must be adapted to accept the vagaries of one or more printing technologies. Variables inherent to most technologies include the placement of each bar, within locational tolerances, and the printing of each bar to its design width, within dimensional tolerances. These factors are particularly significant when printing at the maximum possible density.

Each printing technology has a characteristic resolving power. This is an ability to print a line (and a space) of minimal width wherein the line is held within a given tolerance. But what tolerance? Some bar-coding schemes are formulated on the premise that the tolerance of bar width must be a ± 25%, while others allow ± 50%. Depending on the cause of width variation, this can mean that those bar codes accepting width variations of ± 50% can be printed with bars whose widths are one-half of those which require ± 25%. This is a significant issue when printing at the maximum density. (When comparing the density potential of two different bar codes, the minimum acceptable width of bar which can be used must be considered, as well as the efficient use of bars and spaces.)

Past and current on-line printing technologies—primarily serial impact printing and mechanical dot-matrix printing—are basically sloppy. They are not capable of holding close tolerances at the densities attempted. Serial impact printers have a maximum resolving power of probably around 0.007 inch ± 25%, while the dot-matrix machines are lucky to hold their hammer diameters ± 25% over the reasonable life of a ribbon.

In contrast, the newer electrostatic printers function with great precision. A line width of 0.005 inch ± 10% is possible with these machines on a continuing basis. These tight specifications preclude many of the assumptions basic to most current bar-coding schemes. As the use of electrostatic printers becomes general (as it will), the bar-code art will become more consistent and much more reliable.

Attempts to combine (1) the need for ones and zeros which can be identified with maximum reliability, with (2) the available printing technologies, illuminate various potential bar-coding principles. For instance, Identicon's 2/5-CODE is a straightforward extrapolation of basic principles previously stated, where wide bars are used for ones and narrow bars for zeros.

While the 2/5-CODE wastes the potential of the spaces between its bars, these spaces are put to useful purpose with other coding schemes. In fact, spaces can be utilized by either one of two means. In one, either a narrow bar or narrow space is used to indicate a zero, while a wide bar or wide space is used to indicate a one. In the other, a narrow bar identifies a one and a narrow space a zero, while wide bars and wide spaces—their widths always integral multiples of the narrow bar/space width—are used to indicate short sequences of ones and zeros. In most such codes, the maximum width sequence is four: one, two, three, or four zeros and one, two, three, or four ones.

The previous discussion exercises the concepts of wide and narrow bars and spaces. But how wide is "wide" and how narrow is "narrow"? The answer to these questions depends on whether printing is accomplished at the maximum resolving power of the printing technology used, or at some multiple of that resolving power. (Low-density printing simplifies the processes of both printability and readability.) However, at any density level it is much easier to tell the difference between a wide bar which is three times the width of a narrow bar, than it is to tell the difference between a wide bar which is only twice as wide as a narrow bar. In fact, at the resolution level, it is not possible to tell the difference between a bar or space which is twice as wide as some other bar or space, if the width tolerance is much more than ± 25%. At the same time, it is possible to work with a 3/1 ratio and a tolerance of ± 50%.

In many codes (but not the 2/5-CODE) the dimensions of the light bars (spaces) are just as important as the dimensions of the dark bars. If the ink spreads to burden the positive tolerance of the dark bar widths, the effect on the light bars is to exercise the negative tolerance. In other words, if the dark bars are wider than they should be, the light bars will be narrower than they should be. While an algorithmic assumption can be made that the effect of the ink spread is the same for all dark bars in any one message, this is not necessarily true in all circumstances; the possibility of both plus and minus tolerances in one message does exist and, if it exists, it puts a real strain on the reading algorithm. It is therefore safe to assume that any code based on a 2/1 ratio is less secure than one which insists on a 3/1 ratio.

It is useful to consider the minimum printable bar as a one, and the minimum printable space as a zero, where this bar and space have the same width. Together, these can be called coding *elements*. The actual bars and spaces used in structuring a particular code might then be called coding *components*. In these circumstances, a coding component's width is always an integral multiple of a coding elemental width. Some codes assign "one" and "zero" significance to components, while others assign such significance to elements. Both assignments are valid and can be combined in one code to give maximum read reliability. That is, parity checks can be run at both the component and the element levels.

It should be stressed that both printing technologies, and technologies which transform the space phase of what is printed into the time phase of what can be read, have resolving powers—the ability to print and read a line of minimal width. Together, these elements constitute a system's resolving power. As bar codes manipulate both spaces and lines, a system's resolving power is the same for both.

In computer terminology, each bar-code cipher represents a *byte*—some combination of *bits,* some combination of ones and zeros. There are two very basic different kinds of codes. With *continuous codes* all ciphers end in a zero (a space), while in *discrete codes* all ciphers end in a one (a bar). As discrete codes do not utilize the spaces between ciphers, while continuous codes do, continuous codes have the potential of being more compact. The Material Handling Institute's USD-1 probably puts more ciphers into less space than can be accomplished by any other code. However, a stiff price is paid for this superior density, because continuous codes cannot perform certain tasks possible to discrete codes.

The potential utility of the bar-code technology can be compared to those of both OCR and magnetic stripe in the series Figures 4.1, 4.2, 8.3, 8.4, 9.2, and 9.3 where the advantages and disadvantages of each are listed. These

BAR CODE READING

● ADVANTAGES

— EASY TO PRINT	— INEXPENSIVE MEDIA
— EASY TO COPY	— NON-RESTRICTED FORMAT
— WORD PROCESSING COMPATIBLE	— INEXPENSIVE TO READ
— LOW ERROR RATE	— HIGH SPEED PRINTABLE
— NON-CRITICAL WANDING	— MATERIAL IMPRINTABLE
— FULL CHARACTER SET	— BEAM SCANNABLE

Figure 4.1.

BAR CODE READING

● DISADVANTAGES

— LOW INFORMATION
DENSITY

Figure 4.2.

comparisons are not valid for any one application. Rather they relate to a whole spectrum of applications of interest to production control.

DISCRETE CODES

Thomas Jefferson invented a means of encoding which was used well into World War II. This consisted of a number of paper strips on which the complete alphabet was printed in random sequence with each strip in a set of strips using a different sequence. These slips were laid side by side and then moved laterally, one to another, until the desired plain-language message took shape in some vertical column. Any other column could then be used for the encoding. The process could then be reversed by anyone who had a similar set and knew in what order each strip had originally been used. The same general process can be used to relate bar-coded messages to their human-readable equivalents, providing the bar code used is discrete.

Why would anyone wish to consider such a principle? Bar coding can become a means—an alternate to keyboards—to communicate at the local level with computer systems. But keyboards are inherently discrete and if a nondiscrete bar-coding scheme is used, some bar-coding potential is lost.

Consider one application: Production control can prepare travelers (sheets with information and instructions) in a situation where preprinted messages, printed in bar-code form, can control the format by which an operator in a work station reports progress—provided that particular progress is what is intended. In practice, there are many circumstances where actual performance seldom duplicates intentions. For instance, supposing a work station is directed to produce 500 parts of some particular design; based on a given rejection rate, the actual number produced will doubtless be either more or less than directed. How, then, does the operator report the actuals?

In one scenario, using a chart of individual bar-coded ciphers (posted on the work-station wall; see Fig. 5.9), the operator wands in the desired message, cipher by cipher. (In fact, Intermec's portable terminal uses this technique in its bar-coded keyboard.) This has the disadvantage of a high probability of sequential error. As an alternative, a Jefferson chart (see Fig. 4.3) could be located on the work-station wall. The operator could then slide the elements to represent the human-readables desired, and sweep the bar-coded enciphering in one pass with little fear of error. The disk encoder of Figure 4.4 is an alternative to a Jefferson chart. Otherwise, there must be a keyboard located in each work station. In these circumstances, the hardware cost of a system using a continuous code is—potentially, at least—much higher than the hardware cost of a system utilizing a discrete code. In a

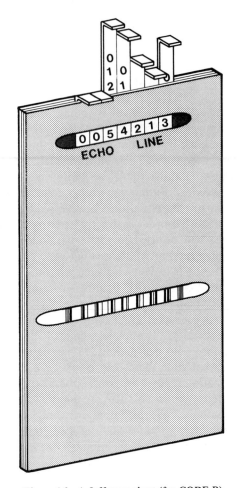

Figure 4.3 A Jefferson chart (for CODE-B).

system which collects data from many places, this can have a major impact on overall system cost.

Reversing the issue and examining it from the other quarter, a practical "poor man's" header printer can be constructed along the lines of the rubber-belt date stamps now found on many desks (see Fig. 4.5). It is only a matter of setting the coded message in the format desired (as the date is now set) and then stamping away, from an ink pad, to one's heart's content. But such a scheme is only possible using a discrete code which is print-forgiving—that is, a four-component code where the wide components are three times the narrows. The 2/5 CODE and CODE-B have this potential—

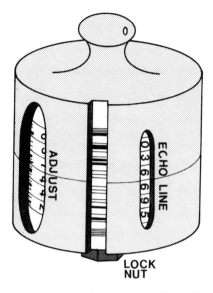

Figure 4.4. A disk encoder (for CODE-B).

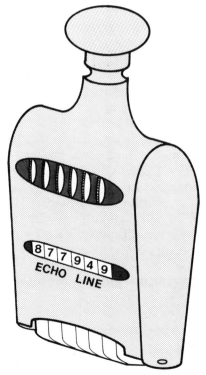

Figure 4.5. A rubber-belt printer (for CODE-B).

they are probably the only codes which do—being discrete codes with a minimum cipher set, utilizing 3/1 coding elements.

The above comments are not made tongue in cheek. Print-quality bar codes are perfectly feasible with such a device. It is possible to maintain a minimum bar width to ±50% tolerances, assuming the rubber stamp is reinked from a pad before each impression. (As an alternative, plastic-tape embossing instruments such as supplied by DY'MO could be used to create messages of any length, albeit of low density.) Comparing the cost (a few dollars) and the print quality (no voids, few spatters, and a print contrast ratio above 85%) to the thousands of dollars which must otherwise be invested in mechanical dot-matrix printers that print with poorer quality, underlines the significance of adopting a bar-coding scheme where it is possible to exercise this option.

COLOR

The chromic factors in the bar-code art include (1) the color of the light used to illuminate a coded message; (2) the color of the ink used to print an encodement; (3) the color of the background upon which an encodement is printed; (4) the color sensitivity of the transducer used to detect light reflected from an encodement; and (5) the color transmissibility of the optical system considered in total—both the path by which illumination reaches an encodement, and the path over which reflected light returns to the sensing transducer. Each of these five factors can be treated as a variable to achieve a variety of objectives, while at the same time creating a number of problems which must be understood and addressed.

An issue of considerable importance is the relationship between the color of the illuminating light (1) and the color sensitivity of the sensing transducer (4). Circumstances would be ideal if the energy from a light emitter peaked at a color (wavelength) which was the same as the peak sensitivity of the sensing transducer. Unfortunately, nature is seldom kind. Figure 8.2 shows the wavelength/sensitivity response of three semiconductor transducers now used in different bar-code scanners: silicon diode, charge-coupled device (CCD), and the particular transductive element used in one Hewlett-Packard wand. From this sketch, a potential problem should be immediately apparent. None of these transducers comes close to duplicating the response of the human eye. When one of these transducers is used to evaluate bar codes, it will not see what the eye sees (or vice versa).

Each type of ink (2) has a wavelength reflectance characteristic which could be superimposed on the chart of Figure 8.2. If this reflectance has a sharp peak at any wavelength, as a colored ink does, it cannot be evaluated simultaneously by both the human eye and any solid state detector (4). Fortunately, the response characteristics of many (but by no means all) black inks are fairly flat from 400 to 700 nanometers; when this is so, the eye and a transducer can work in fair harmony.

At the present time, various commercial devices make use of incandescent, helium/neon laser, light-emitting diode (LED), solid-state laser, and quartz iodine light sources (1). Each of these sources has a wavelength emissivity characteristic which could also be added to the chart of Figure 8.2. The only one shown is a LED designed to peak at 700 nanometers. Incandescent light sources have the advantage of very flat emissivity over a wide range of light wavelengths, but because they supply energy to such a wide range, their efficiency at any particular wavelength is very poor—that is, they take a lot of electrical energy to generate their illuminating energy. In addition, they tend to be somewhat susceptible to shock damage. In any event, their use in scanning systems is fading fast.

Most hand-held wands now use LEDs as light emitters (1). These are quite efficient in transforming electrical energy into light energy, but they function only over a very narrow range of wavelengths. Figure 8.2 includes the response of a particular LED used in one Hewlett-Packard wand.

The spectral-response curves of Figure 8.2 are plotted on a per-unit basis: they indicate the amount of illuminating energy (1) which may be expected at any particular wavelength as a ratio of what is achieved at the wavelength of peak energy. Not shown are absolute magnitudes—or even magnitude relationships—of energy peaks for different devices. This introduces a significant issue, for with current LED technology the efficiency of transform—from electric power to light energy—decreases with a decrease in wavelength. In other words, red LEDs put out more light energy than do green ones, while infrared LEDs are more efficient than visible red LEDs.

From an electronic standpoint, then, with silicon detectors peaking in the infrared (960 nanometers) and infrared LEDs putting out more light, an infrared scanning system appears to offer optimum scan performance. This is true because the more light (1) used to illuminate an encodement, and the more sensitive the transducer (4) in detecting reflections, the more effective the scanning system. Such a system has a maximum amount of information to work with and is less disturbed by optical/electronic distractions.

These conclusions lead to the issue of the ink (2) used in printing bar codes. Here the criterion involved in choosing both inks (2) and background material (3) is one of reflectivity. Some inks (and dyes) have low reflectivities (they absorb the illuminating light), whereupon they look like bars (which is the objective), while others have high reflectivities and look like background. The high-reflectivity inks are called "blind," because their presence is ignored by the transducers (4) contained in read heads.

Unfortunately, most inks are blind to infrared radiation, carbon inks being among the few exceptions. This means that, if infrared scanning systems are used, bar codes must be printed with special ink. This is a serious restriction which can well increase the cost of a scanning system. For instance, if the art work on a package is printed with an ink blind to infrared energy, a bar-code label must then be added, using carbon ink, in a second printing process. This makes little sense, and it is unnecessary when shorter wavelength scanning systems are used.

Then too, carbon inks are very abrasive when compared to many noncarbon inks. They tend to wear out any mechanism (wand, print hammer, etc.) with which they come in contact at a much faster rate than do other inks. In addition, currently available carbon inks seem to be less stable than noncarbon alternatives: they are slow to dry and their tendency to smear is greater. It is a mistake, then, to commit a program to an infrared scanning system, because of the ink problems associated with this choice.

An ideal system would scan with green light because this fits best with the human eye. But there are no efficient green light sources, so a compromise is in order. A common compromise is visible red light (630–700 nanometers). Most laser scanners used to scan bar-coded messages are based on helium-neon gas which lases at 633 nanometers. An ideal ink absorbs more than 85% of all of the 633 nanometer light energy to which it is exposed.

But suppose a given label is to be both laser-scanned and wand-scanned during various stages of its useful life. Certainly, under these circumstances, a wand should ''see'' that label in a manner at least similar to the way a laser views the situation. As discussed above, if a wand can still see the printed ink, then the longer the wavelength of its light source is, the higher the potential efficiency of its electronic circuitry. Considering the variables of ink reflectivities and LED emission efficiencies, plus the 633 nanometer laser constant, many hand-held wands now on the market operate at around 700 nanometers. While the reflectances of most inks are not the same at both 633 and 700 nanometers, these points are close enough to allow reasonably cohesive performance.

To use an infrared wand and a helium-neon laser scanner in one system is to ask for confusion; visible red should be used throughout. While specific measurements are required for each ink of interest, as a general statement, black bars on blue or green backgrounds are not easy to read with scanners operating in the red portion of the light spectrum, while the same bars on yellow, orange, or red backgrounds can be read without much deterioration of print contrast. In other words, when using a monochromatic red light source, red looks white, blue looks black, and orange, yellow, and green appear in varying shades of gray, green being quite dark gray.

Copies of bar-coded labels can be compromised through the utilization of dark red backgrounds. Here, red looks white to the scanner but black to the copy machines. (In fact, it is possible to read bar codes in a black-on-black context if the background is all blind, the bars are printed with carbon ink, and scanning is accomplished at infrared wavelengths.)

Color coding is a commonly used and very valuable means of communicating with humans by rote. Both messages and stock can be color-coded as a means of directing transactions. When scanning with red light, black, blue, and green inks can be printed on red, pink, orange, and yellow stock. As many forms are preprinted with green ink, care must be exercised not to print a bar code label over a green line, since the line will appear black to the scanner and the label will not be read properly.

PRINTABLE LANGUAGE

Bar codes are a printable language. As is true for all other printable languages, their utility lies in an ability to organize documents in whatever format best communicates the originator's intent to the recipients. The next chapter discusses various applications and particular document formats that achieve this objective.

5. Documents

Bar-code concepts received an early impetus as a part of efforts to facilitate, expand, and record point-of-sale descriptions. While success was achieved in this, it is a limited application in which all relevant items can be labeled well in advance of their use in any transaction of interest. Identification objectives can be met with labels preprinted in batches. Such batches can be structured so that labels are incised with the same information, sequentially indexed or created in coordinated sets. Labels so printed can be drawn from stock and affixed to their federated items at any convenient time. With these objectives, an organization utilizing this technology does not need to operate its own printer. The required labels can be ordered well in advance of their use at reasonable prices from any number of vendors. Even if an individual in such an organization wishes to print his own labels, a variety of printing devices capable of off-line batch operation can be purchased or leased.

In contrast, manufacturing transactions place a much greater burden on the labeling art, because identification problems are more varied and relatively complex. While in this environment some labels can be batched in anticipation of use, others must be created on demand, utilizing information randomly drawn from computer memory. In these latter circumstances, label printers must be operated in real time. The demand for real-time labeling is a major difference in concept between systems designed for monitoring manufacturing transactions and those designed for point-of-sale transactions.

DOCUMENT TYPES

There is a significant logistic difference between documents (see Fig. 5.1) which are printed in batches and those which are created on demand. As noted in Chapter 7 on "Print Technology," batch printers can justify a much higher hardware cost than can demand printers. In a production control environment, travelers are commonly printed in high volume at a central location, while floor documents are created on demand, in low volume, at many locations distributed over the production area.

DOCUMENTS

- TRAVELER
  - — BATCH
  - — HIGH VOLUME

- FLOOR
  - — DEMAND
  - — LOW VOLUME

- FRISKET
  - — DEMAND
  - — LOW VOLUME

- CUT SHEET
  - — EDGE INSERTED

Figure 5.1.

Several organizations are now printing as many as ten thousand travelers each working day. These move out from their central location and perform their diverse functions at many locations in many transactions. Under this load, the cost of a traveler printer is of small consequence. Here the priority is getting out travelers printed fast in high quality.

At the same time, various documents (friskets, move tickets, added headers, and the like) must be created on demand out on the factory floor. These documents are commonly put to task in locations more or less in the general vicinity of the places where they are created. Here the required printers are not used much, but a large number are needed; hardware cost is a major concern.

TRAVELER

In many organizations Production Control prepares a packet containing both information and instructions, as a basic means of launching a project on the production floor. The skin sheet for such a packet is identified by various colloquialisms including *shop ticket, work order,* and *traveler.* Such a document moves (travels) through productive structures, carrying whatever information is required to initiate desired productive acts. Here a traveler both directs each transaction of interest, and uniquely identifies each task when job status is communicated back to Production Control.

Travelers are commonly created in batches at central locations, often at Production Control's headquarters. A very flexible approach is used when travelers are prepared on conventional dot-matrix page printers. Here the headers for any sized documents are printed in a machine-readable bar-code format, with the rest of the document available for anything else. "Anything else" covers a lot of territory. Many organizations are now using 8½ × 11 inch, or even larger, 100# card stock for travelers. Here the bar-code header is printed along with a great deal of human-readable information.

The above discussion describes a whole class of documents, commonly utilized by Production Control, which can be batched on page printers. Only recently have relatively inexpensive, mechanical dot-matrix printers become available. As these printers provide the only way of printing the required documents, on line, at a low enough cost, it is their availability which has made integrated bar-code programs practical. As a result, it is this availability which is a major factor leading to a rapid adoption, industry wide, of bar-code labeling programs.

The Renk traveler of Figure 5.2 achieves a high level of sophistication which takes full advantage of the bar-code art, combining any quantity of human-readable information and any quantity of machine-readable information with a format which is completely flexible. A document of this type represents an entire unit of work divided into its constituent operations. This work unit is identified by a header which encodes the job order number. Further, each individual operation is bracketed by a START and a COMPLETE transaction where each such transaction is fully identified by a bar-coded message linking in a series the JO#, the OP#, and either START or COMPLETE. An operator in a work station need only read the concatenated message, which represents the job status, by sweeping a bar-code wand across the bar-coded symbols. Time and location are added automatically to give a complete description of a relevant transaction.

This concept offers four features not otherwise available. First, it gives Production Control much tighter control over the way performance is reported. By concatenating all the relevant information, it eliminates the possibility of mistakes in a lengthy keyboard manipulation. Second, assuming the wand incorporates some kind of feedback feature in its design, it eliminates the need either for a personal terminal in the work station, or for the operator to leave his work station in order to use a work-center terminal. This feature can have a tremendous effect on the overall cost for an extensive system. In other words, document sophistication can be used to offset hardware cost.

Third, the concept presents the whole work unit in an orderly, progressive flow wherein information may be provided in such detail as to make unnecessary other sources of information. The traveler then becomes the entire packet instead of merely functioning as the skin sheet for a number of other documents. (Some Renk travelers are said to be as much as 20 feet long!)

Finally, other bar-coded messages can be added between the START and COMPLETE transactions. For instance, bar-coded instruction can be in-

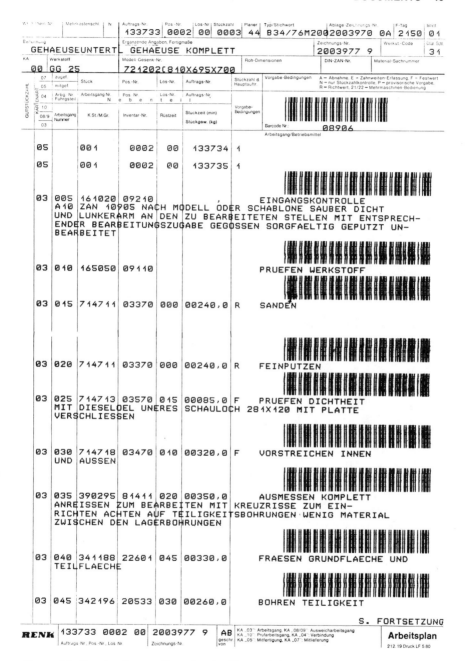

Figure 5.2. Traveler format. Reproduced with permission of Zahnraderfabrik Renk Aktiengesellschaft.

cluded for operation setups. This addresses still another source of potential error. Or, if the job order and operation numbers (plus a code designator) are concatenated in a short message printed to the left of the traveler, but in line with the "complete" message shown on the right, that information can be used to report aberrant conditions which cannot be anticipated in advance. As one example, if a traveler called for the fabrication of 500 parts and only 483 were completed, that fact could be reported by first sweeping the JO#OP#D and then adding the *4, 8,* and *3* from a chart posted on the work station wall. After that, the operation would be closed with the COMPLETE message.

POSSIBLE TRAVELER FORMAT

1. HEADER

A *header* identifies a document. In this example, the document relates to a particular job order number: JO# 0159616. The first digit, here a zero, is the check cipher. A header can be scanned to determine the current validity of any document in question.

2. OPERATION

By concatenating job order number (0159616), operation number (15), and status (here a *6* is used to indicate START), a full status report is accomplished merely by scanning one message. In these circumstances, time and location are added automatically. The spacing between a START and a COMPLETE is as flexible as anyone might wish: any amount of human-readable information can be included here.

COMPLETE:

(Here a *9* is used to indicate COMPLETE.) Note that the check cipher is now a *1.*

3. *INTERRUPTED OPERATION*

* 1 0 1 5 9 6 1 6   1 6   6   *

* 1 0 1 5 9 6 1 6 1 6 S *

If one adds a message (above on the left) consisting of the job order number (0159616), the operation number (16), and a "flag" (here an *S*), a report from some other source can be injected between START and COMPLETE. This might be a menu chart hung on the work station wall (i.e., "machine down," "parts shortage," actual quantity, or the like).

COMPLETE:

* 0 0 1 5 9 6 1 6 1 6 9 *

4. *INSTRUCTED OPERATION*

* 0 0 1 5 9 6 1 6   1 9   6   *

* 0 0 1 5 9 6 1 6 1 9 S *

If one adds still another message, instructions can be bar-coded. In the example below, a particular instruction (6660155) is used to configure an instrument of some kind located in the work station.

* 0 S S 6 6 6 0 1 5 5 *

COMPLETE:

* 1 0 1 5 9 6 1 6 1 9 9 *

MOVE TICKET

An item leaving a work station moves to a floor-control staging area of some kind, from which it should move to a second work station at some later time. Or, with a little luck, an item might move directly from one work station to another without pausing in a staging area. In either circumstance, some kind of document is commonly associated with each item to supply information in both human-readable and machine-readable forms relevant to the movement.

Conceivably, movement might be directed by information carried on Production Control's traveler. But in the long run, movement direction is a prerogative of floor control's in situ processes and cannot be temporally directed by a document prepared in advance. While the information supplied by such a document is limited to move-requirements, it must be provided in both human-readable and machine-readable forms. It is a document characterized by very little information.

If an item is in a tote box, and movement is to be accomplished by forklift, a move ticket might be tossed into that tote box. It should then be possible for a forklift operator to decide what to do with the tote box, without having to leave his vehicle to examine the instructions close at hand. Human-readable characters are then printed in alphabetic symbols large enough to be read from a distance.

A move ticket is a document intended for a very short-term use, printed on site, on demand, in low volume. Move tickets can now be printed on conventional matrix printers in any desired format.

LOG

Printers are available which read bar-coded messages preprinted along one edge of a "slip" or card, and add transaction descriptions to that card in the form of a sequentially printed log (see Fig. 5.3). In systems utilizing these printers, the bar-coded message accesses a memory which supplies both the text to be printed and the position on the card where the text should be printed.

As these printers operate on documents inserted into a slot, documents of any size can be serviced, provided only that their format is responsive. For example, work-station activities can be logged on a traveler at the same time that they are entered into computer memory. Under these circumstances, the traveler carries a complete history of the project to date which can be perused by floor management without having to access computer time.

LOGGER

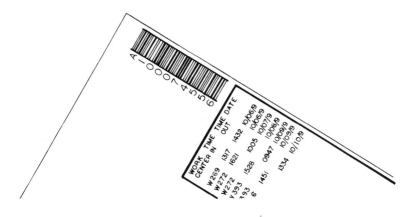

Figure 5.3.

TOTE-BOX LABEL

Tote boxes on mechanized transport systems—as for example in queue on carousel—require some means of machine identification in order to control the routing function. The only requirement is a unique identification number which can be used to address a look-up file. The look-up file will then establish what is in the tote box, while the tote-box label identifies the tote-box location. This application is a natural for the bar-code art. Numerically sequenced labels can be batched off-line and affixed to each tote box where they can be beam-scanned at strategic locations dispersed along the transport system.

CUT-SHEET HEADER

In the interest of integrating one labeling technique throughout one organization, consideration should be given to the various cut-sheet documents prepared by various segments of that organization: correspondence, bills, expense statements, purchase orders, and the like. A bar-coded header can be printed on any of these documents by the same printer used to print the text on these documents at the time of original preparation. By the application of appropriate firmware an entire document, both header and text, can be prepared as one unitized increment of effort. (In contrast, the magnetic-stripe technology would require affixing an adhesive label, which is both expensive and logistically absurd.) Copies of bar-code headed documents can be prepared on many of the document copy machines—Xerox, IBM, Kodak, etc.—where the header is just as easy to read on a copy as on the original.

Further, organizations must process many different kinds of documents prepared at locations outside their control: purchase orders from customers, correspondence, bills from vendors, receipts, shipping lists, and the like. Just as when those documents were originated, so in this instance it is not economic to affix adhesive labels of any kind in order to provide them with a machine-readable header. Rather, it should be possible to insert these documents into the slot of a slip printer whose bar-code print capability is determined by some kind of dot-matrix print head. Such a printer would then print the desired header along one edge of each cut sheet.

ENCASED DOCUMENT

Much is made in some quarters of an ability to read information from magnetic-stripe documents through layers of dirt, grease, and other non-magnetic contaminants. While such a contention is demonstrable, it may well be irrelevant in practice—at least to a degree. As stressed previously, travelers (and other documents involved with human-readables) are burdened with human-readable as well as machine-readable requirements; it profiteth naught to read the one without being able to read the other. If grease can contaminate the machine-readables—so that, as the logic goes, magnetic stripes are desirable—that same grease might also obscure the human-readables, so that the characteristics of magnetic stripes would be of no help whatsoever. Such a document is useless!

In short, much can be argued for the characteristics of labels of the magnetic-stripe genre: they can be read through grease! But the same logic serves no purpose when applied to travelers. The only practical solution, then, is to enclose such a document in a protective cover like a plastic envelope. If the plastic is transparent, if the bar-coded label is printed with due consideration of the application, and if an appropriate choice is made of reading hardware, both the machine-readable and the human-readable information can be read through the plastic cover without undue deterioration of read quality.

Here, magnetic-striped documents are impractical. They must be removed from the envelope in order to make a machine reading. Magnetic stripes present such a short depth of field that they cannot be read through a cover more than 0.003–0.004 inch thick. As such a cover is much too thin for envelope use, the technology is not available for this purpose.

PICK LIST

With lives at hazard, appropriate medication or other treatment must be directed to particular patients. Given the tremendous variety of drugs now available, the institutional character of most medical facilities, and the questionable legibility of many doctors' handwriting, it might well be wondered whether any exposed human can long survive. Certainly the potential for error inherent in such a system can be lethal. Perhaps the answer lies in bar coding.

As shown in Figure 5.4, catalog sheets can be bar-coded in duplication of the labels which identify the containers used for most medical products. Now doctors can prepare their prescriptions (pick lists) from catalog sheets by using bar-code wands.

Once a prescription is printed by a computer peripheral (which document includes within its format a reproduction of the catalog's bar-code message), any druggist's wand can easily rationalize the pick list against the items provided. Here the chances for a mistake are almost eliminated, while at the same time an audit trail is provided. Further, such a document can be used at any time to access archived information in an encyclopedic review of a prescription's historical profile.

The concepts of using catalog sheets to organize pick lists, of rationalizing pick lists against product labels, and of using pick lists to access computer archives extend well beyond anything medical. These same general requirements are duplicated in tool-crib logistics, in the organization of the shipping process, and elsewhere. In fact, a number of organizations are now considering adding bar-coded labels to their catalog sheets to both expedite and maximize the accuracy of their sales orders.

PARTICIPATIVE DOCUMENT

Instead of on card stock or sheets of plain paper, printing can be done on label stock carried by a release liner. Label stock is available in any size and format, where printing possibilities include the services of matrix machines with full graphics capabilities.

If larger objectives are structured into smaller logical parts where each part is identified by a small label, a set of labels (one for each component part) can represent a single document fully describing the larger objective. Such a document generally resembles a traveler, but its functions are somewhat different. As this label-set traveler moves through various work processes, labels are peeled off and affixed to appropriate items—other documents, work pieces, or whatever. All the items so identified

DESCRIPTION	ITEM CODE			BAR CODE
	SSQ	MIN	PACK	
				-TABLETS BEGINNING WITH K
K-LYTE-CL FRUIT PUNCH TABS 30	246-868			
	1		1	
K-LYTE/CL CITRUS TABLETS 30	246-850			
	1		1	
— K-LYTE/CL 50MEQ 30 CITRUS	247-015			
	1		1	
K-LYTE/CL 50MEQ 30 FRUIT PUNCH	247-007			
	1		1	
K-TAB TABS 10MEQ 100	261-339			
	1		1	
KAON-CL TABS 250'S	107-979			
			6	
KAON-CL-10 750MG 100	261-685			
	1		12	
KEFLEX CAPS 500 MG 100'S	025-585			
			24	
KEFLEX CAPSULES 250 MG 100'S	025-551			
			48	
KINESED TABLETS 100'S	026-989			
			1	
KLOTRIX TAB 10MEQ 100	260-950			
	1		1	
KUTRASE CAPSULES 100	229-328			
			1	
KUZYME CAPSULES 100S	215-962			
			1	
				-TABLETS BEGINNING WITH L
LANOXIN 0.125 MG 100'S	062-711			
			48	
LANOXIN 0.125MG 1000'S	134-197			
			12	
LANOXIN 0.25 MG 5000'S	025-122			
			12	
LAROTID CAPS. 250MG 100S	121-228			
			1	
LAROTID 500MG 50'S	074-609			
			1	

Figure 5.4. A pick list. Reproduced with permission of Computype, Inc.

DESCRIPTION	ITEM CODE			BAR CODE
	SSQ	MIN	PACK	
				-TABLETS BEGINNING WITH L
LASIX 20MG 100'S		075-515		
			1	
LASIX 20MG 500'S		148-627		
			1	
LASIX 40 MG 500'S		072-439		
			1	
LASIX 40MG 1000		246-538		
			1	
LASIX 80MG 50		226-068		
			1	
LEDERCILLIN-VK 250MG 1000		072-066		
	1		1	
LEDERCILLIN-VK 500MG 100		072-074		
	1		1	
LEMBITROL 10/25 CAPS 100		197-046		
			1	
LEMBITROL 5-12.5 CAPS 100		197-053		
			1	
LEUKERAN 2 MG 50'S		072-553		
			12	
LEVOTHROID 0.1MG 100		063-420		
			1	
LEVOTHROID 0.2MG 100		063-438		
			1	
LEVOTHROID 0.3MG 100		063-446		
			1	
LEVSIN W/PHENO TABS 100'S		069-401		
			1	
LIBRAX CAPSULES 500'S		023-127		
			1	
LIBRITABS 10MG 100'S		074-138		
			1	
LIBRIUM CAPS 5MG 100		285-353		
	1		12	
LIBRIUM CAPSULES 10 MG 500'S		023-226		
			1	
LIBRIUM CAPS 25MG 100		285-361		
	1		12	
LINCOCIN CAPSULES 500 MG 100'S		052-662		
			1	

Figure 5.4. (*Cont.*)

MODEL
L-22

SERIAL 1022 100E1 71665

DESC   L-22 ORGAN WAL DOMESTIC

VOLTS   115   HZ 60 AMPS 0.87 WATTS 100

1716653

LOWREY®

1716653

MODEL L-22   Finish   WALNUT
SERIAL 1022 100E1 71665

115 Volts A.C.   60 Hz   0.87 Amps   100 Watts

LOWREY Division of Norlin Industries, Chicago, Illinois U.S.A.

THIS ORGAN IS MFG'D UNDER ONE OR MORE OF THE FOLLOWING U.S. PATENTS

3,190,951	3,236,931	3,283,056	3,558,792	3,617,602	3,715,445	3,745,225
3,842,184	3,902,397	3,929,051	3,986,425	4,010,667	4,032,720	4,038,898
4,074,233	4,118,791	4,128,035	4,135,423	4,148,240	4,148,241	4,173,915
4,183,277	4,186,637	4,186,642	4,200,842	4,208,939	4,215,616	4,228,713
4,242,936	4,244,260		OTHER PATENTS PENDING			

CAUTION — TO PREVENT ELECTRIC SHOCK, DO NOT REMOVE BACK. NO
USER-SERVICEABLE PARTS INSIDE. REFER SERVICING TO QUALIFIED
SERVICE PERSONNEL. ATTENTION — AFIN DE PRÉVENIR UN CHOC ÉLEC-
TRIQUE NE PAS ENLEVER LE COUVERCLE ARRIERE. IL NE SE TROUVE À
L'INTERIEUR AUCUNE PIÈCE POUVANT ÊTRE RÉPAREE PAR L'USAGER.
S'ADRESSER À UN RÉPARTEUR COMPÉTÉNT.

1716653

| 1022 100E1 71665 |

| 1022 100E1 71665 |

1716653

| 1022 100E1 71665 |

| 1022 100E1 71665 |

1716653

| 1022 100E1 71665 |

| 1022 100E1 71665 |

CSA®
LR-15417

LISTED
UL® 563H
MUSICAL INSTRUMENTS

Figure 5.5. A Lowrey traveler. Reproduced with permission of Lowrey, Inc.

L-22   1022100E171665 990001022100
WALNUT   115 60 0.87 100

10 L-22
1022 100E1 71665
115 60 0.87 100
WALNUT 990001022-100
1716653
W a r r a n t y — R e c o r d

9 L-22
1022 100E1 71665
115 60 0.87 100
WALNUT 990001022-100
1716653
S h i p p i n g — R e c o r d

8 L-22
1022 100E1 71665
115 60 0.87 100
WALNUT 990001022-100
1716653
I n v e n t o r y — R e c o r d

7 L-22
1022 100E1 71665
115 60 0.87 100
WALNUT 990001022-100
1716653
P a c k — R e c o r d

6 L-22
1022 100E1 71665
115 60 0.87 100
WALNUT 990001022-100
1716653
C o n s o l e — A s s m.

5 L-22
1022 100E1 71665
115 60 0.87 100
WALNUT 990001022-100
1716653
O n H e a t — R u n

4 L-22
1022 100E1 71665
115 60 0.87 100
WALNUT 990001022-100
1716653
M a n u a l — O f f L i n e

3 L-22
1022 100E1 71665
115 60 0.87 100
WALNUT 990001022-100
1716653
M a n u a l — I n L i n e

2 L-22
1022 100E1 71665
115 60 0.87 100
WALNUT 990001022-100
1716653
C h a s s i s — P a n — O f f L i n e

1 L-22
1022 100E1 71665
115 60 0.87 100
WALNUT 990001022-100
1716653
C h a s s i s — P a n — I n L i n e

Figure 5.5. (*Cont.*)

53

automatically become part of a coordinated set whose organization was established at the point of origin by Producton Control.

The traveler of Figure 5.5 was printed on a Printronix 300.

SHIPPING LABEL

By the use of an ink-jet or electrostatic printing press (such as the Mead DIJIT), labels of almost any size and complexity can be batched off-line at high speed with resulting low cost. (This cannot be done with the magnetic-stripe technology.) These labels might be prepared in series, with different addresses on each label, but with a common bar-code message indicating a common content. Or alternatively, the address on each label could be bar-coded. Product and package can be checked by hand-wanding, to be sure the right contents are placed in each package, and the package label can be beam-scanned for address routing, truck loading, and the like.

The shipping label of Figure 5.6 was printed on one of Versatec's NCC–80 electrostatic printers.

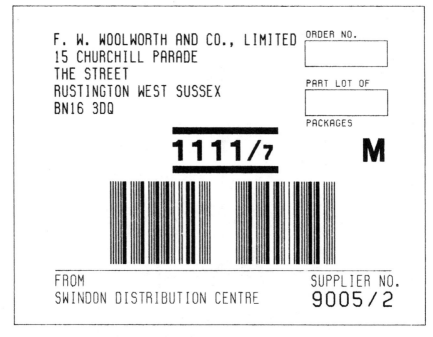

Figure 5.6. A shipping label. Reproduced with permission of Versatec, a Xerox company.

FRISKET

A *frisket* is an adhesive label attached to an otherwise deficient document for the purpose of bringing current the information carried by that document. Let us consider an example of frisket logistics. When a traveler reaches a work station, the operator of that station can query a computer, using the traveler's machine-readable header. If the particular traveler is up to date, the operator can proceed on that basis. But if the traveler is not up to date, the computer responds by printing a frisket. This print-on-demand frisket is then applied to the traveler, and the operator can proceed with confidence in the corrected document. This print-on-demand, on-site concept minimizes the chance of operating with an incorrect traveler.

Frisket printing is, then, an on-site, on-demand process which requires a relatively inexpensive ticket printer capable of creating machine-readable labels. The label of Figure 7.1 was printed on an Intermec 8220.

PIECE WORK RECORD

When an employee is paid for piece work, the work record itself should be left in the hands of that individual. In some circumstances, this is a legal requirement but, even when not dictated by law, it is an expression of wisdom. Otherwise the Personnel Department is likely to become the largest part of an organization.

In one scenario, each worker is issued a card of standard format, identified by a bar-coded serial number as a unique header. This card is divided into a multiplicity of areas the number of which exceeds the quantity of piece work which a reasonable person can be expected to perform in a given accounting period. (Stakhanovites can be issued two cards.) Each of these areas is identified by a message, printed in bar-codese which states "nothing." A participative traveler then moves with the work. This traveler includes within its format a number of peel-off labels each of which is barcoded to identify a particular work unit—a "something." As an operator completes each work unit, he or she peels the appropriate label from the traveler and covers one of the "nothings" on the work sheet of interest with a frisketed message which says "something." At the end of an accounting period, a laser scanner is used to read all the bar-coded information from both an ID card and the work sheet. In a few seconds the complete record of work performed is lodged in computer memory, while the worker retains the original document. In the same manner, each traveler can be scanned at any time in an overview of work which remains yet to be performed.

TICKET/CARD

Security, machine-readability, and various levels of user sophistication (and lack thereof) coalesce in a requirement for an inexpensive technique which can be used to prepare documents carrying messages, represented by a few characters, which uniquely identify each document. Applications include amusement park passes, garment tags, electronic hotel keys, transportation vouchers, ID cards, and the like.

The current focus on the use of magnetic-stripe cards for high security purposes, and the consequential problems associated with that technology, are discussed in Chapter 9, "Magnetic-Stripe Technology," while the inherent shortcomings of OCR are covered in Chapter 8, "OCR Technology." In most applications, bar coding offers a much simpler answer with more read reliability at lower document cost.

Figure 5.7 shows bar-coded labels added to conventional ID cards. If these labels are included under the plastic laminate, it is almost impossible to alter their encodement, since attempts to tamper with the recorded information destroy the card. As a result, the stored information is much more secure than with magnetic-stripe technology—even with magnetic stripes of high coercivity. Copies of bar-coded documents can be inhibited by printing originals with black ink on a red background, or are made almost impossible by printing with carbon ink on a black background blind to infrared light, and then reading the result with infrared light.

The magnetic-stripe coding scheme (for that matter, even the bar coding of Figure 5.7) is limited by a requirement that the document must be moved along a particular linear path, while the stripe is held in close proximity to a reading head. To make this card move along its path calls for a level of decision making by a user which is not generally successful without some learning experience. Figure 5.8 illustrates a concept of Bruce McPherson for a bar-code medium that can be presented to a reading machine where the only limitation is that of having one of the two flat surfaces available to a reader. This is as simple as placing a coin in a vending machine. Printing a bar-coded message on a transparent film allows the reading device to "see" the code from either side. Orienting the bar-code bars at 45° to the edges of the document allows the reader to "see" the code at any 90° increment related to any edge. Such a document can be read by either reflective or transmissive means.

PAPER-KEY BOARD

Keyboards are commonly used to formulate messages which either provide local instruments with their operating instructions or are injected into data-processing systems for delivery to remote devices of one kind or another.

Figure 5.7. ID cards. Reproduced with permission of Toye Corporation and Graphic Laminating, Inc.

With conventional keyboards, each key represents a separate mechanism which is activated by the touch of a fingertip. With a paper-key board, as shown in Figure 5.9, a unique printed bar-code symbol is substituted for each key of its mechanism equivalent. Each of the printed paper keys can be

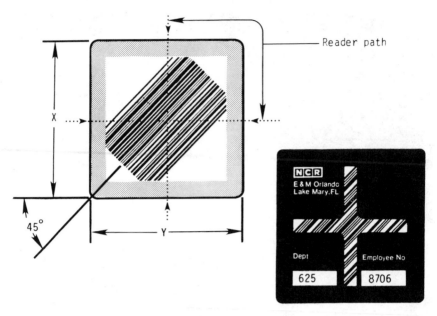

Figure 5.8. The McPherson concept.

wand-swept in a sequence which precisely duplicates the finger-touch procedure.

Depending on the application, a paper-key board might be either advantageous or disadvantageous. Certainly printed symbols are less costly to construct than are mechanisms. Therefore any device which draws on this technology should be less expensive than one using mechanisms. Of perhaps more importance, printed paper keys are less complex than mechanisms of any kind, to the point where their simplicity makes possible instruments which in the long run are more reliable than are their mechanism-driven equivalents.

On the other hand, hand-wanding of a bar-code symbol is a more complex manual process than activating a mechanism with a fingertip. Therefore the issue of paper key versus mechanism key is resolved in terms of a duty cycle: if the keyboard is busy, the instructions diverse, or the messages long, the paper-key board is at a disadvantage.

MENU CARD

In those circumstances where instructions to a system can be served by a relatively short, finite list of possibilities, an appropriately constructed menu rather dramatically eliminates the disadvantage of the paper-key board. By

Figure 5.9. A paper-key board.

formulating complete messages, one swipe of a bar-code wand offers what might well be the fastest possible, most reliable means of data entry.

As shown by Figure 5.10, a *menu card* is a reasonable extrapolation of the paper-key board concept. The significant difference between these two documents is the way they are used. The paper-key board must be read in a series of swipes, one for each character in a message, while a menu, with all possible messages prepared in advance, is read in one pass for a complete message.

INSTRUCTION SET

Keyboards are now used to adjust the operating conditions of literally hundreds of different kinds of instruments. Generally speaking, many of these keyboards are seldom activated. Once an instrument is set to perform as desired, it may continue on this one path without change for a long time. The

SYSTEM	LOAN PERIODS	FUNCTIONS
ACKNOWLEDGE	LOAN PERIOD 1	CHECK OUT
PROCEED	LOAN PERIOD 2	RENEWAL
ACCESS	LOAN PERIOD 3	CHECK IN
REPORT	LOAN PERIOD 4	CLEAR CHANGES
OFF	LOAN PERIOD 5	REFERENCE

Figure 5.10. A menu card. Reproduced with permission of Data Composition, Inc.

process industry's programmable controllers are examples of a class of instrument with keyboards allowing local adjustment that are seldom used because readjustment is rarely necessary. In fact, to prevent tampering with the controls by unauthorized individuals, many of these devices feature a lock-out switch which deactivates the keyboard.

Keyboards are bulky (dictating the size and configuration of a product), their mechanisms are complex (reducing both reliability and environmental tolerance), and they are expensive. Here, then, is an ironic situation—an expensive, seldom-used feature which compromises product design!

Semiconductor circuits now perform many of the functions which in the past were attributed to mechanical actuators. This can be extended to most of the manually operated controls on almost any electronic instrument—even the on/off switch. As semiconductor circuits will accept bar-coded instructions with alacrity, all the front panel controls of most instruments can be replaced by a single receptable into which a bar-code wand is inserted when its services are required. By extending the menu concept, a booklet of bar-coded instructions can be used to program any number of instruments (see Fig. 5.11). This concept is simple, straightforward, and so beneficial in

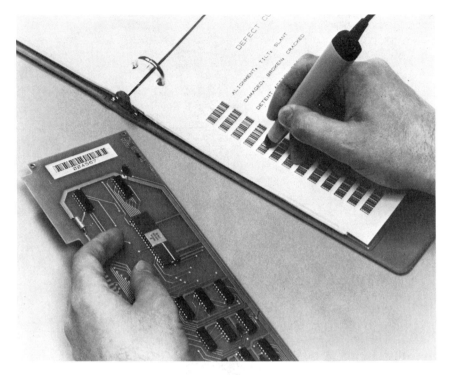

Figure 5.11. An instruction set. Copyright 1981 Hewlett-Packard Company. Reproduced with permission.

all respects that it may be expected, as time passes, to extend throughout the instrument industry—laboratory, factory, field test, and the like. Hopefully, the industry will formulate some effective standards before the technique becomes too pervasive.

PRINTED PROGRAMS

Gutenberg's introduction of the printing press revolutionized the means whereby ideas were passed from one human brain to another. Duplicate books have become so inexpensive and so widely disbursed that almost anyone who makes the effort can find out what he wishes to know. Following logically, bar coding now makes it possible to print computer programs in book form and thereby achieve wide distribution at low cost. Hewlett-Packard pioneered this technique in programming their hand calculator (see Fig. 5.12), while Cassio programs musical instruments from bar-coded

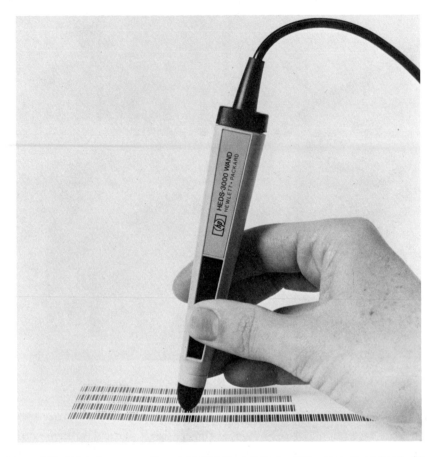

Figure 5.12. Printed programs. Copyright 1981 Hewlett-Packard Company. Reproduced with permission.

scores, and both Western Publishing and Texas Instruments tickle their "talking books" by the same means.

FORMAT SIGNIFICANCE

The format used in composing machine-readable documents can have a profound effect on the cost as well as the reliability of those systems designed to perform both the print and read functions. Consider, for instance, the objective of bar-zipping. Figure 5.13 shows an envelope supposedly sent to West Newbury but which improperly bore Wenham's ZIP. It further shows two different ways in which Wenham's BAR ZIP might be printed. One is based

Figure 5.13. Format implications.

on a horizontally oriented clocked code, while the other uses the preferred code, USD–2, printed in a vertical configuration.

BAR ZIPs are of interest primarily because they make possible the sorting of mail by automated means. In this application, envelopes move in the direction of their long axis through a sorting system where such movement is referenced to each envelope's lower edge. When the clocked code is used, one photosensitive transducer reads the lower clock track as an envelope is moved by a read station, while a second transducer simultaneously reads the upper information track. While such read heads are relatively inexpensive when considered by themselves, they only get one shot at reading each BAR ZIP as envelopes go zipping past. Further, such a BAR ZIP must be printed with fair precision in relation to an envelope's lower edge, to be sure that both clock and information tracks line up with their appropriate read heads.

A linear-array read head for use with the USD–2 code may cost a bit more than two photosensitive transducers, but it will have several chances of reading each BAR ZIP as envelopes dash madly by a reading station. Because of multi-pass reading, the use of the vertically oriented USD–2 code is potentially more reliable than is a single-pass clocked code.

Of perhaps more significance, the location of the face of an envelope of a USD–2 BAR ZIP is not particularly important. In fact, all its benefits accrue as long as the BAR ZIP is organized more or less in the vertical or ladder direction and appears somehow within the view of a linear-array read head as an envelope slips by. In other words, it matters very much where a clock code is printed, while location is of small consequence with USD–2.

The problem illustrated by Figure 5.13 is that of a mistaken ZIP, including a BAR ZIP, which requires correction. Here, in the circumstance of the clock code, the entire message must be erased and printed over with new information. This is likely to be both inconvenient and expensive. On the other hand, with USD-2 it is necessary only to abort the first message and print a second wherever space is available on the envelope.

A USD-2 message is made unreadable merely by distoring the bar pattern in some way. Post offices once canceled postage stamps with inked corks carved to print whimsical figures; perhaps these could be resurrected. But a line drawn by any means, as illustrated, will do the job just as well. This does not cost much.

Clocked codes are special-purpose codes restricted to a few tasks, while USD-2 is a general-purpose code which can be adapted to any task. This fact is underlined by MIL-STD-1189 (which improperly calls USD-3 the 3/9-CODE) and by the increasing acceptance of USD-2/3 for production control use throughout the discrete manufacturing community.

European ZIPs are alphanumeric, while U.S. ZIPs are numeric only. As USD-2 is alphanumeric, it will serve both systems. However, it unnecessarily complicates U.S. ZIPs. Utilizing the general-purpose "tier" concept, the U.S. ZIPs could take advantage of the less complex, higher print-density potential of CODE-B, while at the same time one sorting system would handle any mixture of both codes.

The phrase "general purpose" includes within its meaning both an ability to be read by any means—laser, linear array, and hand-held wand—and an ability to be printed by any means, down to rubber-belt, hand-operated stamps. The latter issue is not unimportant, for how else are individuals going to BAR ZIP their correspondence at home?

The choice, then, is clear: between a restricted clocked code and a less expensive, more reliable, more versatile general-purpose USD-2 (or USD-2/CODE-B, tiered) code. But whatever document format is used, and whatever form of bar code is chosen, the resulting document must be readable according to some practical means. The next chapter discusses relevant reading issues.

6.   Read Technology

Bar-code reading is accomplished by sweeping a small spot of light along some path which intercepts all bars. This includes passing over significant white spaces both before the first bar and after the last bar. As a bar code cannot be read if the traverse wanders outside the barred area, bar heights are chosen to maximize the probability that this will not happen. Physically longer coded messages generally call on the services of bars of greater height. Here the bar heights should be at least one-sixth the message length. Light-spot scanning can be accomplished by either manual or automated means. Figure 6.3 lists the major options.

The information contained in bar codes is highly redundant (the higher the bars, the greater the redundancy). In other words, the information contained in a coded message is available along every path which fulfills all reading requirements. If one path traverse does not yield a reading, it is only necessary to try again along some other path. This process can be repeated indefinitely until a reading is obtained. While repeats may be a bit inconvenient with manual scan, they can be programmed to take place automatically for high-speed light-beam scans.

Reading bar codes involves several factors. First, the area containing a printed message is illuminated by a spot of light. The diameter of this light spot should be about the same dimension as the width of the narrowest spaces between bars or the width of the narrowest bars. Second, the light reflected back from an encoded area is sensed. If the light spot falls on a bar, the reflected light should be minimal. If the light spot illuminates the space between the bars, the reflected light should be maximal. From this difference in reflected light, it is possible to tell whether the light spot illuminates a bar or a space.

Third, the light spot is swept through a path which intercepts all the bars and all the spaces of a complete coded message. The reflected light from the swept illumination is then sensed as a pulse-width-modulated light-intensity signal, wherein the received information is contained in the pattern of modulated light. This pattern is a temporal duplication of the spatial bar-space distribution pattern. This intensity-modulated light is then detected by a photo transducer and converted into a voltage characterized by pulse-width modulation. Figure 6.1 illustrates a spot of light moving along a path which crosses a cipher representing the character *9* in USD–2.

The bar/space patterns of bar codes are organized following various mathematical data-processing principles to achieve various objectives. These principles include the following: the information contained in the reflected light modulation is rejected by the electronic circuits of the reading instruments unless it contains a fully recognizable legitimate message; the light spot can be scanned across a message in either direction; there is a clearly recognizable difference between the different bar widths and between different space widths; and the light spot can be moved over a wide range of different scanning speeds.

The diameter of light spots used in bar-code scanning must be chosen to achieve pulse-width modulated signals of optimum configuration. If the light spot is too large, both the leading and the trailing edges of the modulated voltage pulses will not be clearly defined, and the electronic circuitry will have difficulty deciding just what it is trying to read. Figure 6.2 illustrates how the signal quality deteriorates when a message is scanned by a light spot of too large a diameter. Smaller light spots give cleaner electronic signals when bar codes are laid down with high-quality printing and a low noise background. However, the light spot diameter can actually be somewhat larger than the smallest code component and still give readable signals.

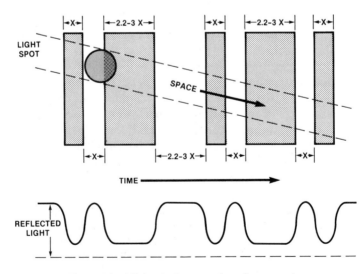

Figure 6.1. A light spot's conversion of space to time.

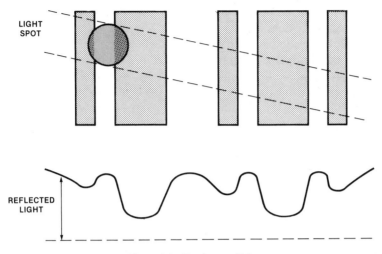

LIGHT
SPOT

REFLECTED
LIGHT

Figure 6.2. Too large a light spot.

Figures 6.1, 6.2, 7.4, and 7.5, considered together, give some idea of the effect of spot size on signal quality. If a light spot is too small, reflections obtained will be modulated by small spot contaminations in the spaces between bars, small voids in print quality, and even variations in print surface texture. All such extraneous signals are viewed as noise by reading instruments. If the noise level is too high, the electronic circuitry will have a difficult time making a reading.

Figure 7.5 illustrates the effects that dark spots between bars and imperfections in bar density have on the quality of the electric signal which is obtained in a sweeping traverse. If these imperfections are significant enough, the cipher cannot be read. When printing is accomplished in the presence of optical noise, larger light spots are required to reduce (even out) that noise. These larger light spots, in turn, enforce the lower coding densities required to maintain modulation quality.

Electronically speaking, fast scanning of low-density codes has the same effect as slow scanning of high-density codes. As long as the noise level is low in both circumstances, a wand whose resolution (spot diameter) is adequate for a high-density code will work just as well in reading low-density codes. The effect of irregular bar edges is not the same as noise. Bar-edge placement determines the relative timing of the leading and trailing edges of the pulse-width modulated voltages. This timing must fall within certain tolerances; if the bar edges are irregular, the code density must be reduced to the point where the irregularity falls within these tolerances. While both noise and bar-edge irregularity are compensated for by lower coding densities, the presence of noise requires the use of large light spots in the scanning system, whereas bar-edge irregularity does not.

In USD-2, two wide bars and three narrow bars are associated in each cipher, with the spacing between bars arranged in a pattern of three narrow spaces and one wide space. The narrow spaces and the narrow bars should be of the same width, while the wide spaces and the wide bars should also be of a common width which is three times the width of the narrow components. If these criteria are not met owing to some defect encountered along a scan path, that cipher will be rejected by the electronic circuitry and the message will not be read. It then takes two compensating defects to create a substitution—one to make a narrow bar look wide, and another to make a wide bar look narrow. Even under these circumstances, if the spacing requirements are distorted, a substitution will not take place. In industrial environments USD-2's SER is nominally less than one in one million, when a "check" cipher is included in the message.

When using manually operated wands to read messages, it is a fairly easy task for a human to move his hand at a constant velocity without giving the matter much thought at speeds of between 3 and 50 inches per second. Below 3 inches per second, it is difficult to maintain the required constant velocity and, when exposed to significant acceleration, the electronic circuits tend to lose track of what they are supposed to be doing. Speeds above 50 inches per second require calculated effort, and for that reason their possibilities have little value.

In fact, most manual reading is carried out at velocities in the range of 10 to 30 inches per second, where the higher and lower limits merely provide a margin of safety. As long as the maintenance of wanding speed does not require conscious effort, it really does not matter what speed is used because, in fully manual systems, the transaction rate is not determined by wanding speed but rather by what happens in between the wanding of two different messages.

There are two time intervals of interest to bar-code reading: the length of time a system takes to read a bar-coded message, and the length of time taken to digest what has been read (the decoding time). Most systems accept readings rapidly without much thought. With laser scan this can be as little as 1/800 of a second. While some systems digest at an acceptable rate, others take seconds to decide what they have read. In some applications, seconds between readings do not matter very much, whereas other applications are sorely compromised by such a delay. Thus, if a tool-crib attendant is releasing a kit of tools against an authorization list, a two-second delay between each reading would be most inconvenient.

Where wanding involves the activities of only a single hand and there are other functions to be performed between readings, as in the circumstances of reading labels affixed to bins, manual wand movement is a reasonable method of operation. However, manual wanding of a large number of cut-sheet headers is a two-handed process where one hand moves or holds the sheet while the other moves the wand. Here reading speed is limited by an awkward paper shuffle which can be smoothed out by eliminating the manual wand and using an automated beam scanner of some kind (see Figure 6.11). In such a system a document is introduced into the scanning beam by either a one- or a two-hand cycle, whichever is faster and more convenient. With a beam scanner, the document read rate can be improved from about one every two seconds to possibly three per second. Perhaps speed is not the issue here: beam scanning is simply more convenient and less tiring than wand scanning.

High-speed beam scan becomes a major issue when there is relative motion between the label and the reading station, as with moving railroad cars or items on a moving assembly line. In such applications bar-coded labels are commonly read at relative velocities of 500 feet per minute (six miles per hour). Even this speed can be increased somewhat by increasing the bar height (in the direction of motion) proportional to the speed desired. In fact, speeds as high as 40 miles per hour have been read with success.

HAND-HELD WAND READING

A bar-code wand, or light pen, both focuses a beam of light on bar-coded surfaces and senses reflections from them. There are a number of different kinds of wands now on the market with widely varying characteristics in terms of emitted light frequency, optical configuration, electronic circuit philosophy, code-density resolving power, and mode of operation.

Incandescent bulbs are supplied as light sources in some wands. These radiate energy over a broad frequency spectrum which can be used to il-

BAR CODE SCANNERS

- TIP JEWEL WAND
- LIGHT SHROUD WAND
- OPTICAL FIBER WAND
- INTEGRATED WAND
- LASER BEAM
- NONLASER BEAM
- LINEAR ARRAY

Figure 6.3.

luminate messages printed with almost any kind of ink and read with almost any light transducer. While these characteristics are desirable in this application, heat-energized filaments consume a great deal of power and tend to break if such a wand is dropped or otherwise unduly shocked.

In other wands, incandescent bulbs are replaced by LEDs: light emitting diodes. These are very rugged, solid-state devices which emit light at only one frequency while consuming minuscule amounts of power. For some time highly emissive low-cost LEDs were available to operate only at infrared (IR) frequencies. At these frequencies many commonly used inks are invisible (blind), and high carbon inks are required to give adequate print contrast ratios (PCRs). More recently, VR–LEDs (visible red LEDs) have been applied to the wand art. While these limit the choices of inks to some degree, they are not as restrictive as are the IR–LEDs and do not require carbon inks.

Bar-coded messages are read by moving a read head in a sweeping traverse. Most bar codes respond to a wide range of different sweep velocities. However, whatever the velocity used, it must be kept more or less the same over the full traverse. A significant change in sweep rate encountered during a traverse is likely to abort a reading. With an automatically programmed sweep, the chance of a velocity change is not a problem. But with manual scan, longer messages are harder to read because it is harder to maintain a constant velocity over the full length of a message.

TIP JEWEL WAND

One popular type of wand features a ruby sphere embedded in its tip. This tip jewel functions as (1) a wear surface, minimizing wear of both wand tip and encodement; (2) a filter, eliminating spurious optical noise such as that generated by fluorescent lights (but not sunlight or arc welding light); (3) an aperture closure, to keep the optical path free of obstruction; and (4) a lens which both delivers an illuminating light spot and recovers reflected energies.

Tip jewel lenses focus the required light spot at a particular point which is very near to the jewel's surface but not on that surface. As a consequence, when a wand jewel is in contact with a coded surface, the wand focuses on the code only when the wand axis addresses that surface at some specified design angle. If the wand attitude exceeds some critical angle, the illuminating and recovered energies no longer relate to the code pattern, and coded messages cannot be recovered. (The lens's focal point is lifted off the coded area by the spherical surface of the jewel.) Further, if the wand angle is less than some critical angle, the light spot is focused at some point in back of the coded surface, the resolving power is dissipated, and the message cannot be read. Some wands are designed for optimum performance when used at an angle of 25° from the vertical. Figure 6.4 illustrates two angles for this type of wand. With one angle the delivered spot size is optimum: the diameter of the spot is the same as the width of the minimum code component. With the other, where the wand is held vertically to the coded surface, the spot is much too large for satisfactory reading. Obviously, various factors such as first read rate and substitution error rate are functions of the wand attitude angle. Because read performance (as well as velocity of scan) depends on how the wand is held, it is not possible to claim optimum performance in an extensive bar-code system where many individuals are using wands at many different angles.

The tip of any bar-code wand must be open optically, so that light can get out and reflections can be recovered. But a wand whose tip is open physically tends to clog with material picked up in the process of scanning, which obstructs the light path. As a result, a regimen of repeated cleaning is necessary—particularly under dusty or dirty conditions. This can be a real chore. In this type of environment, the tip jewel performs yeoman's service by making it relatively easy to keep the tip clear of optical obstruction.

However, this leads to a classical dichotomy of two less-than-desirable choices. As the tip must be open optically, it must either be open physically or be closed with an optical element. If the tip is closed with an optical element, as with a tip jewel, that element will wear and, in the process, the wand's performance will deteriorate. As the spherical shape of the tip jewel is altered by wear, the scanning light spot increases in diameter, whereupon the first read rate falls off while the substitution error rate increases.

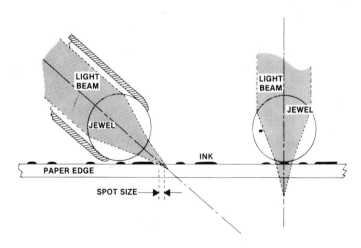

Figure 6.4. A tip jewel wand.

As a tip jewel wand's performance is dissipated through use, one must ask at what point the wand needs to be replaced because its performance is no longer acceptable. In an installation where several hundred wands are at play, this can be a very sticky issue.

The red material from which a ruby is constructed passes infrared light while blocking visible light. This "low pass" filtering action very neatly takes care of the wildly fluctuating fluorescent lights (but not sunlight) by restricting the reflected light to infrared frequencies. However, the use of an infrared filter means that the illuminating light must be infrared. As many inks do not absorb infrared energy, this imposes a requirement that barcoded messages, to be read by such a wand, must be printed using carbon (or other IR-absorbing) ink. This can be a serious restriction, since carbon-ink-impregnated fabric ribbons have several unfortunate characteristics: the carbon in the ink is abrasive, engendering wear on any mechanical part which is exposed; documents tend to smear, because carbon inks are sticky and slow-drying; and the dimensions of bars and spaces vary unacceptably over the life of a ribbon, because carbon inks tend to spread more with a new ribbon than do certain noncarbon alternatives.

All wand tips wear with use, as both ink and paper are abrasive. While a tip jewel may well last longer than any other wear surface, wear on the jewel represents permanent functional deterioration. Other wands have replaceable tips. The wear on these also represents performance deterioration, but these tips can be replaced easily and inexpensively, returning a wand to its original condition.

The negative aspects of the tip jewel wand include the requirement to use carbon inks; the short depth of field which limits reading through thick plastic envelopes; the restricted angle by which a wand must address a coded surface; the possibility of cracking a jewel; and the difficulty of judging performance against wear. These aspects offset the advantage of ease of cleaning.

LIGHT SHROUD WAND

Figure 6.5 shows a different type of wand where the contained light beam is designed to focus on the coded surface when the wand is held at right angles to that surface. As shown in this figure, such a wand lifts the light spot off the coded surface if it is tipped too far from perpendicular. In this type of wand the tip acts as a shroud which limits reflections from extraneous light sources, including sunlight and welding arc light as well as fluorescent lights.

The issue of depth of field can be important in manufacturing environments where documents may be enclosed in transparent plastic envelopes designed to protect them from dirt and grease. It should be possi-

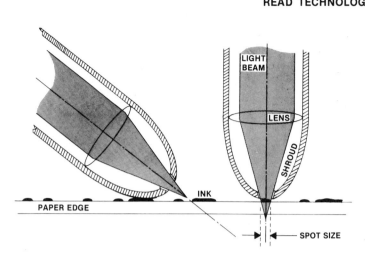

Figure 6.5. A light shroud wand.

ble to read messages through these plastic sheets. As the sheet thickness lifts the wand tip above the coded surface, a reading cannot be accomplished if the sheet thickness is greater than the wand's depth of field. The greater the depth of field, the less readings will be affected by sheet thickness. As the focal length of the optical system used in the wand of Figure 6.5 is much longer than that of the wand of Figure 6.4, it has a much greater depth of field (up to 0.02 inch); this type of wand is likely to be much more successful in reading through plastic covers.

However, when reading through transparent films of any kind, this wand cannot address the film surface at right angles, because surface reflections obscure anything beneath that surface. As a result, the wand of Figure 6.5 must be tipped at least 15° from normal when reading through films. As this same wand cannot be tipped beyond some other angle, this restraint makes the wand reading angle much more critical; wanding can be accomplished only with greater operator care.

OPTICAL FIBER WAND

In one wand of recent design by Welch Allyn (shown in Figure 6.6), the problem of reflections from the surface of plastic covers is neatly circumvented through an application of fiber optics. Here the read area is flooded by light introduced at an angle to the wand axis via the optical fibers. The reflected light is then sensed (as a spot) along the wand axis. When the illuminating energy is injected at an angle, the effect is that of cross-lighting. Here reflections from a shiny top surface are sent off at an angle which can be separated

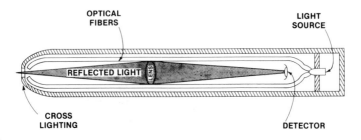

Figure 6.6. An optical fiber wand.

from the reflections obtained from the undersurface encoded with bars and spaces. Such a wand easily reads through plastic envelopes down to the documents so encased.

In this design, a good part of the available energy (light) is used to illuminate a large area of which only a portion—the spot—is evaluated. This means that the signal-to-noise ratio of the reflected energy is not as good as it might otherwise be, if all the light were concentrated in the sensing spot.

INTEGRATED WAND

Hewlett-Packard offers a wand (see Fig. 6.7) which accomplishes cross-lighting by cocking both the light-source axis and the light-reflection axis at angles to the wand axis. Because all the emitted light (all the energy) is concentrated onto the read spot, the ultimate signal-to-noise ratio of the pulse-width-modulated output voltage is maximized.

This wand does quite a good job of reading through plastic covers (envelopes) much more than 0.012 inch thick. Furthermore the light source, optics, light-sensing transducer, and logic electronics are combined into a

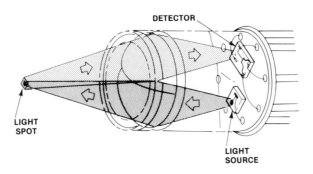

Figure 6.7. An integrated wand.

single assembly which is used as the basis of design by several other wand suppliers.

LASER BEAM READING

In automated systems a beam of light of requisite diameter and intensity is directed at a coded surface from a source which lies at some distance from that surface. A laser beam is sometimes used in order to take advantage of its small light-spot diameter which persists over considerable distances (its depth of field). This light beam is rapidly scanned through some scan angle which, when projected onto a coded surface, traverses a complete message. As light beams can be scanned at high rates of speed, it is possible to scan every message many times over a number of different scan paths. Multiple scanning maximizes the chance of achieving a reading.

This technique has an amazing ability to discriminate between coded messages and complex backgrounds. For instance, laser scan can be used to read the labels on windows of moving automobiles, as well as labels on printed circuit boards moving through various manufacturing environments. A laser beam searches out labels which intrude into its scan angle and makes a reading when it finds one. Otherwise, it ignores what it sees. Commerical laser beam readers are available which scan at a 400 hertz rate. Using these devices, a complete bar-coded message is read in 1/800 of a second.

As shown by Figure 6.8, a laser scanner is characterized by a scan angle, a

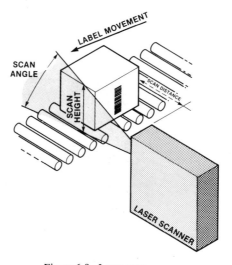

Figure 6.8. Laser scan.

light-spot diameter at a particular scan distance, and a scan height at that same distance. Spot diameters of 0.020 inch at scan distances of 18 inches are available. This indicates a capability of reading messages utilizing USD–2 printed at a density of 3.5 ciphers per inch.

While instruments with scan distances of up to four feet are currently offered, these may depend on messages printed in lower cipher densities. Bar-code labels have been read using laser scan at distances exceeding 20 feet. Here distance readability is enhanced by laying down a retroreflective background onto which the bar-code ciphers are printed.

LOW-COST BEAM SCANNING

It is somewhat inconsistent to automate a means of key bypass by an instrument which requires manual manipulation. Here, the wand's raison d'être is its low cost and rugged construction; hand movement provides a means of low-cost scan traverse.

When studying the interplay of documents and products as they move through various manufacturing processes, one soon finds that it is not always convenient to use a hand-held wand to manually scan identifying labels on each of a large number of documents or other small items. This process is manually awkward and relatively slow.

Of course laser scanners are available, but they tend to be large and expensive. The main reasons for using lasers is to take advantage of their great depth of field and their high-intensity light spot. Where a short read distance can be held reasonably constant (as in reading documents), smaller and less expensive nonlaser optical systems would do the job. Here, the scan head can be held in some fixed position where it is necessary only to intrude the labeled items into the scan path, where the label is read many times.

Figure 6.9. A laser scanner. Reproduced with permission of Scope, Inc.

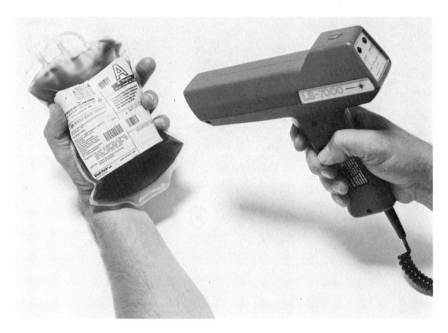

Figure 6.10. A hand-held laser scanner. Reproduced with permission of Symbol Technologies, Inc.

Figure 6.11 illustrates an instrument which continuously scans a space longer than any message to be read, located in the plane of the desk top. Cut-sheet headers can then be read by merely sliding a labeled sheet along the desk top until the header intercepts the scan path. With such a device, message reading can be accomplished at very high speed by an electronic semiconductor array such as that shown in Figure 6.13. When using such an instrument as a miniature computer terminal, the reading process can be controlled by both visual and aural feedback in the form of red, yellow, and green lights plus an audible "beeper." Various signal combinations of light and sound would then provide operating instructions as well as indicate operational status.

LINEAR ARRAY

The image of an entire bar-coded message can be projected, by optical means, onto the sensitive surface of a linear array of transductive elements (see Fig. 6.13). If a bar-coded surface is flooded with light, and the transducer outputs are sampled in turn, the effect is the same as scanning

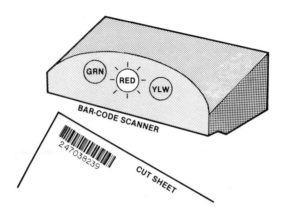

Figure 6.11. A bar-code scanner.

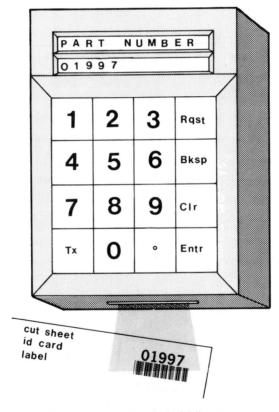

Figure 6.12. A work-station terminal with linear array scan.

Figure 6.13. Linear array. Reproduced with permission of EG&G Reticon, Inc.

the bar-coded ciphers without physical contact or relative motion between ciphers and read head.

In their *C*harge-*C*oupled *D*evice family Fairchild offers just such arrays, extending from the CCD-111 with 256 elements to the CCD-142 with 2,048 elements. While their sensitivity peaks at about 800 nanometers, there is enough sensitivity at 700 nanometers to avoid the requirement of printing the bar-coded messages with carbon ink. If it is assumed that three CCD elements are needed to read each bar-code element, and CODE-B consumes 10 elements per cipher while USD-2 consumes 16 elements per cipher, then these results follow:

	Number of Ciphers in Message			
(CCD elements)	*256*	*512*	*1,024*	*2,048*
CODE-B (Less S/S)	7	15	32	66
USD-2 (Less S/S & C)	2	7	18	39

If the projecting lens is focused to read a bar-code element of 0.007 inch (as printed on an Intermec serial impact printer), the maximum length of message which can be encoded for reading with a 2,048 element array, is 4.5 inches. The maximum number of ciphers which can be printed on a Printronix (0.020 inch elements) is 14 for USD–2 and 22 for CODE–B. While electrostatic printers, soon to come on the market, will improve this performance, it is still adequate for existing printers whose performance extends between that of the Printronix (at 0.020″) and the Intermec (at 0.007″).

Figure 6.12 suggests the design features of a terminal which can perform all basic work-station functions while being completely sealed against environmental contaminations.

FIXED-DISTANCE READING

If the distance between a labeled surface and a read head can be kept constant by some form of mechanical constraint (for instance, as in Figure 6.11), a reading device configuration is possible where the read head and the label need not be in physical contact. Here it is merely a question of a conventional optical system which relates the bar-coded surface and a sensing element at their mutual focus distance.

Where the labeled surface moves, as in a slot reader (see Fig. 6.14), only one transducer is needed in the scan head. If relative motion is not conveniently arranged, the scan head can contain a linear array.

MECHANICAL READ

Some of us are old enough to remember when the gentry, living on the "other side" of town, enclosed their front yards with white picket fences. What a joy it was to run along one of these fences, banging a stick against the pickets, hoping to be out of sight before the irate owner made it to his front door! Doubtless the inspiration for the phonograph came to young Tom Edison following just such an exploit.

Bar-coded messages too can be read by a simple adaptation of this basic operation. If the bars of a bar-code message are either raised above or set below a background surface, an appropriately designed force-sensitive hand-held wand (a stick) will detect the pattern with all the assurance of which an optical scanning device is capable. Such a wand is simplicity personified. Either a piezoelectric or a magnetostrictive transductive element is the only component needed. As these generate their own output voltage, no power supply is required.

Applications abound: raised ciphered serial numbers on tire sidewalls;

Figure 6.14. A slot reader. Reproduced with permission of Computer Identics Corporation.

type designators cast as an integral part of distributor caps; bars die-struck into engine blocks; the etched art work of printed circuit boards; laser engraver tracks; and even printed labels, if the ink is thick enough.

READ ENVIRONMENT

Compared to the alternatives, such as mechanically operated keyboards, the bar-code technology makes possible the collection of more accurate information, in less time, using less expensive hardware. As all of these benefits can be achieved in fairly hostile industrial environments, the prospects are very attractive to those interested in collecting information in work stations throughout the discrete manufacturing community. While work-station activities cover a wide range of possibilities, the ability to read bar codes by either manual or automated means can be used to address most applications. Figures 10.1 and 10.2 illustrate two automated processes while Figure 6.15 shows a typical warehouse where data are collected with a hand-held wand.

Figure 6.15. A bar-code system. Reproduced with permission of NCR Corporation.

PRINT TO READ

The bar-code technology in general involves a requirement to print what is to be read as well as an ability to read what has been printed. While many past bar-code aficionados concerned themselves only with reading what someone else had printed for them, many applications now require active printers as well as busy readers. The next chapter discusses the consequences of various means of printing.

7. Print Technology

A number of different print technologies have been used to print bar codes when the information needed to print such codes is drawn at random from the archives of digital computers. These include: serial impact printers, mechanical dot-matrix printers, ink-jet printers and electrostatic printers (see Figure 7.2).

In the past, bar-code ciphers (and their associated characters) were printed by utilizing various types of serial impact printers. Both drum and band mechanisms have bar-code printing capabilities. Current printers of this type will print only relatively small items—tickets, labels, and tags fed from coiled stock.

One specific device of this kind prints three lines from a continuously rotating drum. As shown in Figure 7.1, one line prints ciphers for USD-2, a second line prints the associated human-readable interpretation of USD-2 in OCR font "A," while the third line provides an opportunity for free text. Because the bar-code cipher and its associated character are printed from the same drum position, there is practically no circumstance under which code and text can be different. In this machine, USD-2 is printed with a density of 9.4 ciphers per inch with a bar height of 0.3 inch and a minimum bar/space width of 0.0075 inch. As shown in Figure 7.3, Esselte Meto offers a hand-held serial impact printer which can be used to print bar codes.

At the other end of the speed scale, preprinted documents of almost any size with serialized bar-code labels can now be run on various electronic "printing presses" with "programmable image" capabilities. Versions of these presses have web velocities of between 200 and 2,000 inches per minute, allowing them to turn out small labels perhaps a thousand times faster than with serial impact printers and at lower cost. But while such devices are economic in the creation of large-sized batches of serialized labels or documents, they are priced far out of range for use as on-line computer peripherals.

● **BAR-CODED LABELS**

Figure 7.1. Serial impact printed labels.

PRINTERS

● **SERIAL IMPACT**
● **VERTICAL MATRIX**
● **HORIZONTAL MATRIX**
● **INK JET**
● **ELECTROSTATIC**

Figure 7.2.

DOT PRINTING

The concept of composing pictures from multitudes of polychromic dots, brought to its epitome by Seurat, is familiar to every art lover. The recognition that characters—or even figures of any kind—can be constructed from dots, and that the placement of these dots can be programmed from computers, is of more recent origin. When it finally became apparent that dot printers (in contrast to fixed-font printers) were not tied to any particular set of characters, a horde of dot-printing devices was commercially introduced. Each component of this horde can be firmware-programmed to print in any language by any means of writing, be it Kanji, Farsi, or Arabic.

At the present time, according to a study of the U.S. Postal Service, over

Figure 7.3. A hand-held printer. Reproduced with permission of Esselte Meto, Inc.

one hundred different organizations are offering mechanical dot-matrix printers, of various configurations, for this purpose. In these instruments, dots are placed on paper as a consequence of mechanical blows delivered from a bank of hammers (print wires, etc.). Here a perceived objective is a graphics capability based on an ability to lay down ink dots in matrices of at least 200 dots to the inch. In this sense, a "graphics capability" assumes that such a printer will completely blacken a page, or provide anything less than completely black which may be desired.

While a Seurat painting is best viewed from a distance, bar-code ciphers must be evaluated at close range. Therefore, each bar is constructed from a series of overlapping dots where the amount of dot overlap is important. As shown by the left-hand bar of Figure 7.4, if the dots of the vertical array used to construct a bar do not overlap by some adequate amount, the transform from space to time depends on the scan path. Here, if the scanning spot passes between two dots, a reading is not accomplished. However, this potential problem is easily taken care of by the dot overlap of the middle bar.

Moreover, the dots of the horizontal array used to construct a bar's width should overlap by 50 percent. With any other dot overlap in this direction, it is not possible to build a bar-code cipher in the highest possible density otherwise consistent with the diameter of dots used.

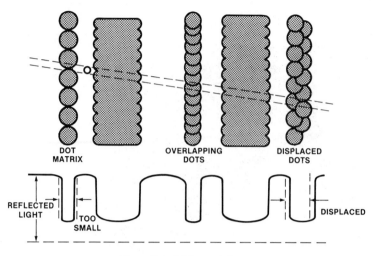

Figure 7.4. Mislocated dots.

Further, in mechanical dot-matrix printers a print hammer is scanned back and forth over the surface of a recording medium. Because of this lateral movement, a dot printed from one such hammer blow is slightly displaced in the direction of hammer scan. If two adjacent dots are scanned from opposite directions, their displacements are oppositely directed. Part of this displacement is a consequence of lost motion in the scan mechanism, but part is also a function of medium texture whereby the softer the media, the greater the displacement. The line of dots displayed to the far right in Figure 7.4 illustrates this phenomenon.

While Figure 7.5 applies to all print technologies, it is a useful print-defect companion to Figure 7.4. Here, if the bars are not uniformly black, and the spaces uniformly white, the information collected by a scan pass will include noise. The amount of such noise affects both the first read rate and the substitution error rate.

OPERATORS

Some mechanism or other—here called an operator—is required for the placement of a dot on a recording surface. This might be a hammer, a stylus, a nozzle, a beam of light, or the like. As with a laser beam, one operator can be swept back and forth (a "flying spot") across a medium of interest, leaving in its wake a train of dots (equivalent to computer bits) in appropriate locations. While a laser beam can be swept with a spinning polygonic mirror,

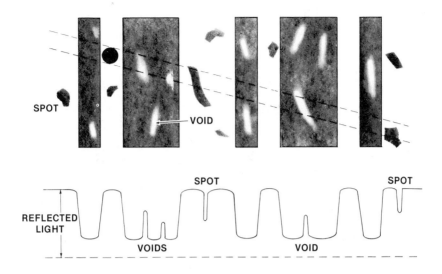

Figure 7.5. Spots and voids.

as in some printers, there is no practical way of moving a single mechanical operator with anywhere near a useful speed.

At the other extreme, a comb of operators (functioning as a "superbyte") can be used to locate every dot on a page without recourse to any mechanism activities other than that of paper travel. For an eight-inch-wide record this requires 1,600 operators! Not only does this number require burdensome quantities of electronics to drive all the comb's teeth, but the quality of printing may be compromised by the vagaries of paper motion.

A number of printers now on the market combine the concepts of "comb" and "flying spot" within the confines of one character. In some of the printers having a bundle of wires in their moving print-head, a single character (whose maximum height is the length of wire bundle) can be printed without regard to any paper movement. Here the electronics need only support one character at a time. However, as regards any printing beyond the confines of one character, the lost motion of the moving print-head, and the factor of paper movement, compromise the performance of such a mechanism when operated in a graphics application.

A few printers combine the concepts of "comb" and "flying spot" within the confines of a line. As in the Printronix machines, several tooth positions (where the teeth are missing) are covered by oscillating one tooth over the distance otherwise assigned to the phantom teeth. By this means, the "comb" of the superbyte is made much less complex, and the supporting electronics are simplified. However, paper movement still affects print quality.

HAMMER BLOW PRINTERS

Typewriters capable of creating "letter quality" documents, and serial impact printers utilizing raised-character drums, commonly print from dry carbon ribbons. These devices are fixed-font printers where each character is laid down in an individual, serial sequence. In a conventional typewriter the ribbon is interposed between the paper and a mechanically driven hammer; the font is a part of the hammer face. In drum printers, the font is a part of the drum's surface, as that drum is positioned in front of the paper with the ribbon held between the drum and paper. The carbon side of the ribbon is presented to the paper, while the backside of the paper is struck by a hammer.

In both the above circumstances, individual characters (each fully formed) are applied to the paper in a single blow delivered against a previously unused portion of the ribbon. That portion which has been so used is completely exhausted (for all practical purposes) and the ribbon is indexed forward by one character width, in preparation for the next blow. As the ribbon can be used only once, the cost tends to be high.

The print quality derived from such a ribbon is expected to be uniform, because no portion of the ribbon is used more than once. However, uniformity depends on constant deceleration of the hammer stroke. As this adjustment tends to wander, the reliability of the mechanism demands close attention.

Inked fabric ribbons can be positioned within printers in much the same configuration as dry carbon ribbons. Here too, hammer blows drive ink from ribbons onto sheets of paper. However, the performance of fabric ribbons differs sharply from that of dry carbon ribbons, because an ink-impregnated fabric functions as a reservoir of sorts. That is, after the blow of a hammer drives ink from a ribbon, the struck portion of that ribbon is only temporarily incapacitated. Because the impregnating ink is semiliquid, it will spread back into a denuded spot, hence that portion of a used ribbon can perform over and over again until all the surrounding ink is consumed. The transport of a fabric ribbon is then organized to give a used ribbon time to recover its ink supply (seeping back from surrounding areas) before it is called upon to function again. This mechanism is used in a wide range of printing devices, including most of the mechanical dot-matrix machines now on the market. It is a clever idea which has been in use for a long time and is now the basis for a tremendous market in replacement ribbons.

Given the objective of a line to be marked by a hammer blow through an inked ribbon, two process variables require consideration. In one, the amount of ink forced from the ribbon by a given hammer blow can vary greatly, depending on whether the ribbon is new or used. In the other, the amount of ink forced from a ribbon depends on the characteristics of the hammer strikes, which in turn are a function of hammer deceleration. Not only do hammer decelerations have tolerances to be considered, but their operating points tend to wander over the life of each adjustment.

NONIMPACT PRINTERS

As a general statement, printing is a process whereby a material (ink) of one optical characteristic is moved selectively from a source onto a printable medium—primarily paper—of a second optical characteristic. Printing is accomplished by manipulating ink particles through a series of steps, each of which can be described in terms of the energy form involved.

Energy exists in five major subforms: chemical, thermal, electrical, mechanical, and radiant (electromagnetic). These subforms can be put to various printing tasks, including the movement of ink particles by force fields. Force fields utilized by existing printers are mechanical (as in hammer blows), electrical, and magnetic:

First, the chemical nature of a photographic emulsion is altered through interaction with electromagnetic radiation (light). The chemical image so formed is translated into an optical image by a chemical development process. Generally speaking, photographic media offer the highest possible print speed. Bell & Howell now sell a device which prints at a paper transport speed of ten feet per second.

Second, there are papers which change color when exposed to an elevated temperature for a sufficiently long period of time. While such materials tend to operate at a fairly slow speed, the required printing mechanism is simple mechanically, consumes a minimum of power, and requires no renewable "ink" supply. As a result, these media are popular for portable, battery-operated devices. The permanence of a record made on heat-sensitive paper is questionable, as an image may easily be erased if exposed to a high temperature for a long enough period of time.

"Teledoltos" paper has long been offered as an "electro-sensitive" medium. It is heat-sensitive where a silver-colored overlay is burned away, leaving a black mark in its wake.

Third, in its colorless "carbon paper" NCR offers a medium which can be marked by mechanical force. Minute particles of a colored ink are individually encapsulated within a film of white material. Mechanical force is used to rupture the capsules, exposing the colored ink against the white film background.

Fourth, a number of patents have been issued for operations in which a colored ion is moved by an electric current from one side of a medium to the other, but none of these appears to have been brought to commercial practice.

Fifth, as in the circumstance of Versatec and Benson printers, an electrostatic image is laid down directly on a special paperlike medium. Electrostatically charged ink particles (of opposite polarity) are then selectively attracted to the image-containing medium to form the desired record in optical form.

Sixth, liquid ink squirted from a nozzle may be broken up into a mist of more or less uniform droplets. In fact, this mechanically disruptive process actually puts an electric charge on some of the droplets. Putting the nozzle in an electric field provides a more uniform mixture. Unfortunately, in such a process there will always be some "wolf" drops which do not collect the intended charge or do not represent the design mass, hence do not go where directed.

High-speed printing presses are now on the market whose operations are based on electrostatic charges selectively placed on the individual particles of an ink "mist." However, only a small percentage of these particles can be used in one print cycle. For economic reasons, then, the bulk of the ink must be recirculated and represented for a following print cycle. The requirement of ink circulation, and the presence of wolf spatters, mean that the hardware cost is inherently high and the print quality is not quite what one might desire.

Both Silonics and Siemens have marketed printers where minuscule droplets of liquid ink are individually ejected from nozzles under computer direction. The ability of a nozzle to perform reliably in this mode is a function of the viscosity of the ink used: the smaller the nozzle bore, the lower the viscosity required. Those inks now used have viscosities which bleed badly on many plain papers. As a result, the so-called "plain" paper which will work with this process is very special indeed.

A conglomerate of solid ink particles is sometimes called a *toner*. It is much easier to form uniform solid particles than to expect a nozzle to generate a uniform mist or eject uniform droplets. Once solid particles are formed, their characteristics should prevail through a number of differently energized printing steps. Solid particles do not change dimension with evaporation and are relatively easy to preserve from contamination. (Solid wolf particles can be eliminated in the manufacturing process and need not show up in the printing phase.) Further, in some printing processes, at least, only useful particles are removed from the conglomerate and the bulk toner does not need to be recirculated.

In existing copy processes and the various printers derived from them, the toner particles are of micron size. They are given an electrostatic charge so as to be attracted to an electrostatic charge of opposite polarity, which is laid down on the surface of either a special dielectric paper or an intermediate medium such as the surface of a dielectric drum. In the Xerox process, the toner particles are transferred from the surface of a drum to plain paper in a high-voltage electrostatic field. When these particles are fused at high temperature, not only will they adhere to plain paper, but they spread out with very little, if any, increase in line width.

This process has been based on fixing the toner particles to paper by thermal fusion. It has long been recognized that a fixing station based on heat is an inconvenient complexity in paper movement (because it must take place down-stream from the print station) and that it consumes a great deal of power. (Also to be noted are the dramatic consequences which accompany paper jams under heat sources!)

Dennison, 3M, and Markem have each developed printing processes which purport to drive dry toner particles into the interstices of plain paper through the application of pressure. Their varying degrees of success are open to some question, when a record so created is exposed to environments of widely varying humidity. Nevertheless, these processes are capable of printing with precise dimensions, as illustrated by Figure 7.6.

QUALITY

How is print quality best defined? First, it is obvious that there must be contrast between a printed mark and the background against which that mark is printed. Here, the print contrast ratio is a measure of the light reflected from

Figure 7.6. An electrostatic printed label. Reproduced with permission of Markem, Inc.

the background, minus the light reflected from the mark, divided by the light reflected from the background.

But quality is also a function of that minimum width of line which can be printed with confidence on the media of interest. Here then is a problem, for this minimum is a function of media texture: the minimum tends to become wider as the media becomes coarser. Nevertheless, there are certain features of a printer's design (and the ink used in such a printer) which can be deduced from the print quality desired.

For the sake of argument, let it be said that the minimum width of line which can be printed on plain paper is in general 0.0025 inch (2–3 thousandths range). But if a uniform pattern is to be printed, the space module (the minimum achievable distance between lines) must have the same dimensional capabilities as the line module (the minimum width of line). This means that, in a dot-matrix printer of any kind, two adjacent inked dots must overlap by 50 percent. If the overlap is other than 50%, the space and line increments will be different. At the very least, a significant incremental difference for these two modules precludes the printing of bar codes at maximum density. From this configuration, the maximum dot density has a distance between dot centers which is the same as the printed dot diameters. If the final dot diameter is assumed to be 0.0025 inch, these dots must be printed on 0.0025-inch centers and the maximum dot density is 400 to the linear inch or 160,000 to the square inch.

Dot-matrix character printers are concerned with dot location only in terms of all dots which go to make up one character. The visual appearance of each character is important, requiring accurate dot placement within a character, but the spacing between characters is not nearly as important and does not need to be held to the same tolerances.

On the other hand, when the dot technique is expanded to full graphics—and to bar-code printing in particular—the location of one dot in relation to all other dots on a page becomes important. In fact, if the task assumed is that of drawing a line only 0.005 inch wide, can dot placement stray as much as 0.002 inch without distorting that line beyond visual acceptance?

The concept of print contrast ratio has been defined previously. Certainly quality printing requires a PCR of better than 85 percent. But quality is also a matter of uniformity of print contrast. The trailing edge of one document should look like its leading edge, and each document should resemble every other one.

Much of the current literature states that bar-code printing is acceptable down to a print contrast of as low as 50 percent. Of course this figure has nothing to do with the theory of bar coding in general. Rather it is derived from the characteristics of the various printers and reading devices used in today's bar-coding programs. It is a statement of the vagaries of today's printing technology, and not the desired technology, or the technology of tomorrow. One must always make do with what the world has to offer, but when it comes to printers, the real world is changing very fast: printers will shortly be on the market which can reliably maintain a print contrast ratio of better than 85 percent. In fact, while their cost remains high, current laser electrostatic printers now print with high print contrast and tight dimensional tolerances.

Low print contrasts tend to lower the first read rate and raise the substitution error rate. As offered now, a low-end specification is merely an arbitrary statement on the part of someone as to the level of read reliability he is willing to accept. Someone else may not be as easily satisfied and may well seek a higher print contrast in order to enhance the performance of his system.

MODE

The way a printer is used, its mode of operation, depends on its application. Each mode has different economic implications. The cost of an expensive printer is justified when documents are created in batches—where a large number of documents, one following the other in continuing sequence, is created at one location. Here a dominant economic factor is the cost of printing each individual document. As a significant portion of this cost may well involve the computer time needed to drive the printer, speed is a matter of prime importance.

Batch printers must be heavy duty machines where accurate paper transport at high speed is a design feature. Applications appropriate for batch printers are characterized first by a central location. The documents created at this location flow out to many peripheral points where the various functions which dictated the creation of the documents are performed. The value of all of these functions, performed at all locations, are summed and related to printer cost. Mailings, inventory run-outs, and travelers (in the manufacturing milieu) are examples of batch operations. Any printer costing more than a few thousand dollars (and some are in six figures) must be considered in terms of its effectiveness in the batch mode.

In contrast to batch printers, a demand printer must be available at the location where the functions directed by the documents it creates are performed. The cost of a demand printer is related only to the value of the functions performed at this one location. Demand printing tends to be intermittent, with the printer performing at a rate which may well be equivalent to light duty. Airline tickets, teleprinted messages, "move" tickets, and hotel bills are examples of demand printing operations.

Demand printing involves the removal of each document from the printer at the end of each demand cycle. The physical configuration of a demand printer's design must therefore include the feature where the tear-off line and the print line are within a fraction of an inch of each other. If this is not so, media waste is a significant factor.

Slip printers are a subset of demand printers. They do not carry their own paper supply; rather, the document to be printed upon is introduced to the printer by hand. Restaurant chits, bank statements, and time cards are examples of slip printing tasks.

Slip printers accept manually introduced documents, move them automatically to desired print lines, print on those lines, and automatically eject for manual disposition. While slip printers do not maintain their own paper supply, they do include rudimentary transport systems in their designs to accomplish the above functions. In addition, some slip printers provide means for both document and print-line identification.

A cut-sheet header printer is a slip printer which will print from only one position. However, several lines may be printed at that position. Here a document is introduced into a slot, the desired printing is accomplished without media movement, and the document is removed. Insertion and removal are manual. Addressing envelopes is one task which can be performed on a well-designed header printer.

Placing machine-readable headers—primarily bar-coded labels—on documents of every kind (letters, engineering drawings, purchase orders, shipping lists, and many, many others) is an application which is just now being considered, but which will ultimately develop into a very large market for header printers. Here an ability to mix human-readable text with bar-coded labels (printed with great precision at the highest possible density) is a requirement.

Figure 7.7 illustrates the basic process of in-line printing. Here the problem solved is that one of placing a bar-code label on each carton passing down an automated conveyor system.

PRINT DEFECTS

Bar-code labels, as a basic part of a machine-readable labeling program, require a higher quality of printing than is necessary for messages to be read by human means. The human mechanism is, in general, more print-quality forgiving than is a probing light spot. Sophisticated and complex systems can be brought to a halt by something as simple (and as common) as a poor quality label. Bar-code labels that fall off, fail to be read on the first scan, or (worse yet) scan incorrectly prevent an automated system from doing its job. Some characteristics of poor-quality bar-code labels include bar-edge

Figure 7.7. An in-line printer. Reproduced with permission of Packaging Service Industries.

roughness, voids in the printed bar, ink specks (or other marks) in the spaces between bars, low print contrast, and susceptibility to surface scratches.

As illustrated by Figure 6.1, bar-coded messages are read by sweeping light spots across coded surfaces. By this means, what is printed—the spatial printed pattern—is transformed into a pulse-width-modulated voltage where the time pattern of this voltage is decoded. As shown by Figure 7.5, voids and specks constitute optical noise which, when transformed into electrical noise, compromise the decoding process.

Figure 7.4 underlines some of the print quality problems inherent with dot-matrix printing. Here a quality space/time transform requires both dot overlap and accurate dot location.

LASER ENGRAVING

There are circumstances wherein it is desirable to imprint messages directly into the materials from which products are fabricated. While this is possible in certain manufacturing processes, laser engravers are fully capable of performing this function with a wide variety of media including metals, plastics, and glass (see Fig. 7.8). Because laser beams can concentrate a great deal of

Figure 7.8. A laser-engraved label. Reproduced with permission of Laser Identification Systems, Inc.

energy in a very small area, high-writing speeds are achieved with this technique. One commercial engraver generates a 0.004-inch spot. This spot is used to engrave a line whose width depends both on the engraving speed and on the rate of heat transfer through the material engraved upon. With steel the minimum bar width is about 0.005 inch, while it is about twice that wide in many plastics.

To be consistent with the reading instruments described in this discussion, the minimum bar/space width should be at least 0.0075 inch. This requires more than one passage of the laser beam when recording on materials with good heat transmission. With this consideration, USD-2 can be printed at a cipher density of 9.4 per inch or less.

There are two types of laser printers now on the market: those which operate off-line through the use of masks, and those which can be driven directly as computer peripherals.

The utility of a product engraved bar-code message depends on the print contrast ratio obtained. This factor in highly variable, depending on both the material printed upon and the laser writing speed. While most bar-code wands require PCRs of at least 50%, this may be difficult to achieve when laser-writing on some materials. However, sometimes there are ways around this problem. For instance, bar codes printed on aluminum and steel have been read with off-axis, laser-driven illumination, in instances where their PCR would otherwise have been much less than 50 percent.

Another possibility—albeit a departure from past practice—is based on the unique features of the 2/5-CODE. This is the only code outlined in Appendix B where the spaces between bars are not a part of the code. As these spaces are not encoded, their absolute widths are not important. Therefore when these spaces—instead of the intervening bars—are engraved, they can be laid down in one pass of a marking stroke. Because the code can be printed with minimal activity, the 2/5–CODE can be printed at a faster rate with a laser engraver than can any other bar code. Further, the resultant "picket fence" of engraved lines can easily be read with a piezoelectric wand without concern for optical print contrast. In many applications, particularly when labeling expensive hand tools, this is an important consideration.

PRINTING OCR

The OCR technology is attractive for two basic reasons. First, the same information is read either by appropriate instrumentation or by human-visual means. Second, individual OCR characters can be printed using conventional typewriters. While ease of printing may be a dominant requirement in some circumstances, a high price is paid for this convenience, as discussed in the next chapter.

8. OCR Technology

The art of using electro-optical instruments to machine-read printed characters which are also human-readable is called *optical character recognition* or OCR. OCR is accomplished in a series of technological steps. First, human-readable characters are printed with light-absorbing inks on light-reflecting backgrounds. Second, the areas which include the possibility of such a printed character are arbitrarily divided into matrices, or grids, of much smaller area that are commonly called *pixels*. Third, each pixel is illuminated. Illumination might be accomplished in time sequence, one pixel at a time, or the entire scanned area can be flooded with light. Fourth, the light reflected from an illuminated pixel is sensed by a phototransducer. As the sampled pixel might or might not contain ink as a portion of a printed character, the amount of reflected light indicates the presence or absence of such ink, hence the presence or absence of a portion of a character. A particular character, then, is identified by a characteristic pattern of ink-containing and non-ink-containing pixels.

The information available to establish identity in an OCR scan is very sparse, and if a significant scob (i.e., pattern defect) is present, the translation from printed character to electronic recognition is blown. As an example, Figure 8.5 shows a *C* and its characteristic pattern of ink-containing and non-ink-containing pixels. It also shows that if the two pixels labeled *X* contained ink, the character would be read as an *O* (or would it be a *0*?). The only difference between a *C* and an *O* is the presence of ink in two pixels! As a consequence, a small speck of dirt can easily introduce a substitution error.

While it is possible (most of the time), to separate *C*s and *O*s under the conditions described above, the discrimination between *O*s and *0*s is much more difficult. The task of discrimination is made much easier by considerable font distortion: each character is shaped as differently as possible from every other character in a character set.

The National Retail Merchants Association (NRMA) has developed two basic OCR font standards. In one of these, OCR–A, machine readability is maximized by making each character's shape as different as possible from that of every other character, without completely losing the appearance required for human recognition. OCR–B was developed as an alternative to OCR–A, because the unfamiliar appearance of the OCR–A alphabet generates a negative human response and, accompanying this response, a consequential deterioration of substitution error in the human-read phase. OCR–B forms are presumed to be more pleasing to the human eye. However, this assuaging of human sensibilities is accompanied by a considerable loss in machine-read reliability, since OCR–B cannot be machine-read with the same assurance as OCR–A. In short, it is really impossible to maximize both machine readability and human readability simultaneously with one character set. As the whole purpose of OCR is to machine-read human-readables, the fact that this cannot be done with high reliability raises some interesting questions about the use of OCR.

Figure 8.6 lists the full OCR–A character set, while Figure 8.1 details the specifications which should be met when printing this set. Included in these specifications are the requirements that a medium printed upon should reflect at least 70% of the light to which it is exposed, while the printing ink should reflect less than 50% of the same light. The light in question depends on the frequency characteristics of the light used to scan a coded area. Figure 8.2 describes the light frequency characteristics of various devices which might be used either to illuminate, or to detect the light reflected from, a pixel. The specifications for OCR–A are based on the use of silicon diode detectors as shown by this graph.

Figures 8.3 and 8.4 list the advantages and disadvantages of the OCR technology when these are considered in the light of a whole spectrum of applications of interest to Production Control.

LASER SCAN

Figure 8.5 illustrates one means of determining the amount of light reflected from every possible pixel. With this technique an illuminating light spot, generated by a scanned laser beam, is swept rapidly back and forth in a vertical traverse whose extent is slightly greater than the expected character height. Simultaneously the vertical scan path is shifted, at a rate somewhat slower than the vertical scan, along a horizontal line wherein the resulting two-dimensional scanning action completely covers the text of a message printed in some OCR font. Such scanning might be performed in a boustrophedon pattern wherein alternate traverses are oppositely directed.

If one phototransducer is used to convert the amount of reflected light into an equivalent voltage, the output signal of a laser-scanning instrument is a pulse-width modulated voltage whose base is a time reproduction of the scan path. Here the minimum voltage values are determined by the passage

RECOGNITION EQUIPMENT INCORPORATED — OCR-A/OCR-B WAND MEDIA SPECIFICATIONS

OCR-A

1. VERTICAL LINE SEPARATION
   0.165″ MINIMUM (4.19MM)

2. TOP/BOTTOM MARGIN
   0.135″ MINIMUM (3.43MM)

3. LEFT/RIGHT MARGIN
   0.095″ MINIMUM (2.41MM)

4. CHARACTER SEPARATION
   0.017″ MINIMUM (0.43MM)
   0.070″ MAXIMUM (WITHOUT SPACE) (1.78MM)

5. NOMINAL CHARACTER WIDTH
   0.069″ (1.75MM)

6. NOMINAL CHARACTER HEIGHT
   0.108″ (2.74MM)

7. CHARACTER SPACING
   8 TO 11 PITCH (.091″ TO .125″)
   (2.311MM TO 3.175MM)

8. CHARACTER MISREGISTRATION
   ±0.020″ (.51MM)

9. MAXIMUM MISREGISTRATION
   0.040″ (1.02MM)

10. CHARACTER SKEW
    ±2° MAXIMUM

11. CHARACTER CENTERLINE HEIGHT
    0.094″ (2.39MM)

12. CHARACTER STROKE WIDTH
    0.008-0.020″ (.20MM-.51MM)
    DEPENDING ON PCS (SEE FACING PAGE)

13. CHARACTER CENTERLINE WIDTH
    0.055″ (1.4MM)

- SEPARATION OF EXTRANEOUS DATA
  - 2 CHARACTER SPACES

- SPECTRAL RESPONSE (NEAR INFRA-RED)
  - RANGE (50% POINTS 730NM — 1040NM)
  - 100% POINT IS 950NM

- MEDIA REFLECTANCE
  - ≥70%

- MEDIA OPACITY
  - ≥85% (RECOMMEND 90%)

- BACKGROUND "SEE THROUGH" OPACITY
  - PCS CHANGE 10% OR LESS

- VOIDS — EXTRANEOUS INK
  .008″ AREAS WITH .040″ SEPARATION

- MEDIA GLOSS
  - ≤60% — TAPPI T-480
  - NON-GLOSSY STOCK RECOMMENDED

- PRINT INK CHARACTERISTICS
  - NON-REFLECTIVE, QUICK-DRYING, PCS ≥50%

- BLIND INK CHARACTERISTICS
  - REFLECTIVE, QUICK DRYING, PCS 10% OR LESS

- MINIMUM LABEL SIZE (NOMINAL DIMENSIONS,
  THREE 10-CHARACTER LINES)
  1.0″ x 1.125″ (25.4MM x 25.58MM)

OCR-B

ALL SPECIFICATIONS ARE EXACTLY THE SAME
AS OCR-A, WITH THE FOLLOWING EXCEPTION:

12. CHARACTER STROKE WIDTH
    MINIMUM STROKE WIDTH IS 0.010″ (0.25MM)
    RATHER THAN 0.008″ (0.20MM)

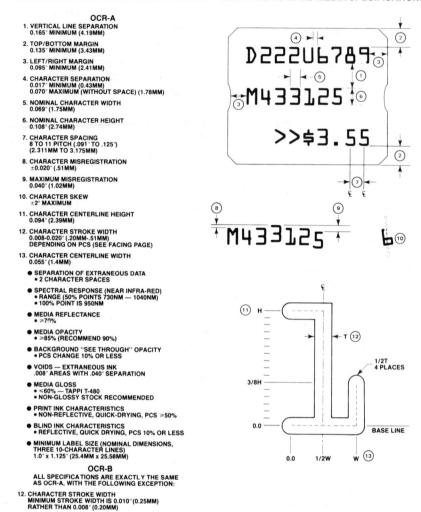

Figure 8.1. OCR media specifications. Reproduced with permission of Recognition Equipment, Inc.

of the light spot over pixels which are fully covered by ink, while the maximum values are achieved by passage over pixels which do not contain ink. The pulse-width-encoded voltage thus generated is then compared to the preestablished pixel patterns for all characters in a set as these patterns are

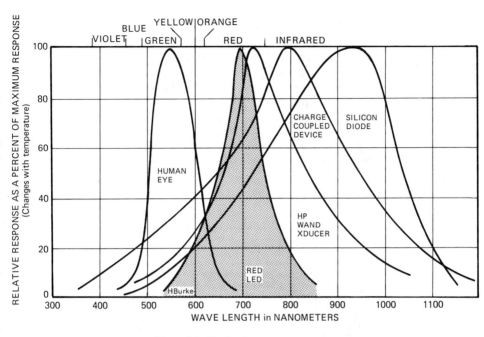

Figure 8.2. Device frequence response.

OPTICAL CHARACTER RECOGNITION

- ADVANTAGES
  - HUMAN READABLE
  - EASY TO PRINT
  - EASY TO COPY
  - WORD PROCESSING COMPATIBLE
  - HIGH INFORMATION DENSITY
  - NRMA STANDARD

Figure 8.3.

stored in a semiconductor read only memory or ROM. The identity of a particular character is established by the comparison process.

(Inherent in this process is the possibility of scanning pixels which are partially covered by ink. When this happens, the voltage pulse heights as well as the pulse widths are modulated. This double modulation significantly complicates the decoding process.)

- ● DISADVANTAGES
  - — EXPENSIVE TO READ
  - — ORIENTATION CRITICAL
  - — RESTRICTED WANDING SPEED
  - — RESTRICTED CHARACTER SET
  - — HIGH ERROR RATE
  - — LOW THROUGHPUT
  - — NOT BEAM SCANNABLE

Figure 8.4. Optical character recognition: disadvantages.

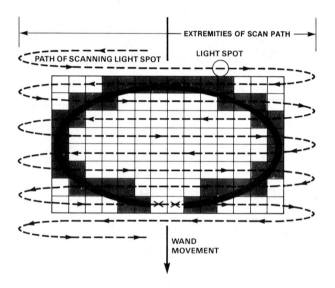

Figure 8.5. A boustrophedon scan.

NRMA STANDARDS

The OCR technology, as directed by the National Retail Merchants Association (NRMA), assumes that the individual characters used to format messages are printed according to rigidly controlled standards. It is axiomatic that nonstandard characters are difficult, if not impossible, to machine-read.

With NRMA standards, each character (see Fig. 8.6) has a nominal width of 0.069 inch (1.75 mm) and a nominal height of 0.108 inch (2.74 mm), while the spacing between characters is held between 0.090 inch (2.29 mm)

FONT	CHARACTER SET	APPLICATION
OCR-A Numeric subset (A)	0123456789 |ⵏ-	Font distorted to maximize machine readability
OCR-A Numeric subset (B)	0123456789 |$.+-	
OCR-A Alphanumeric	0123456789 ABCDEFGHIJKLMNOPQRSTUVWXYZ {}%?&"*+$,.-/'=|;:▪	
OCR-A Numeric	0123456789+,-./|▪	
OCR-A Alphabetic	ABCDEFGHIJKLMNOPQRSTUVWXYZ {}%?&"*$'=|▪:;	
Farrington 7B	0123456789	Used on Credit Cards
E13B (MICR)	0123456789⑈⑆⑇⑉	Used by banks on checks
OCR-B Numeric	0123456789 <>+-/|	Enhanced appearance to human eye
407	0123456789|+$.-/ ▫	
1428	0123456789|./-+H	

Figure 8.6. OCR fonts.

and 0.125 inch (3.18 mm). These specifications create pitches between 8 and 11 characters per inch. In addition, the axis about which each character is printed must conform (within ±2°) to a nominal print axis which is the perpendicular to the line along which a series of characters is printed. Early NRMA considerations of the available technologies resulted in a division of the area, which would cover any NRMA character, into an array which has 9 pixels along the horizontal axis and 15 vertically.

The shape of each OCR-A character, then, is constrained by the format of this array. To the degree made possible by reasonable font distortion, each pixel is either completely covered by ink or is not covered by ink. Thus, the problems engendered by pixels partially covered by ink are minimized by font configuration. The width of line (stroke) used in OCR-A font can give this result if it is either one ninth the standard OCR-A area width $(0.069''/9 = 0.007''+)$ or some integral multiple of that dimension.

Ink is the means by which OCR data are placed on paper. There are basically two types of ink of concern to an OCR reader. These are read ink (OCR ink) and blind ink. Read inks produce a high print contrast—that is, they have a very low reflectance when compared to the reflectance of the paper on which they are printed. When an OCR reader is not able to ascertain any essential difference between the light levels reflected from printed ink and the background, that ink is said to be "blind."

When the OCR technology was first postulated, it was assumed that reflected light would be detected by silicon transducers (see Figure 8.2). These have a sensitivity which peaks in the infrared portion of the electromagnetic spectrum. As a result, the OCR technology is based on the use of infrared light. Figure 8.2 illustrates the significant difference between the way a human views a printed character and the way an OCR scanning device accomplishes the same function.

While the implications of an infrared scanning light are several, the most significant one is the requirement to print OCR characters using a carbon ink. (OCR ink generally means carbon ink.) Most noncarbon inks are blind to infrared light. Carbon inks are highly abrasive (at least more so than many other inks), and they tend to wear out any mechanism exposed to them at a faster rate than would be true for noncarbon inks. In addition, carbon inks tend to smear for some time after printing more than certain other types of inks do. Thus the use of infrared scanning light, which requires the use of carbon inks, imposes what is now an unnecessary constraint on the OCR technology. Nevertheless, it is a part of OCR technology as now practiced.

TRANSDUCER ARRAY

It is possible to organize a number of phototransducers into a two-dimensional array, and to optically relate each transducer of that array to the light reflected from an equivalent grid pixel of the NRMA standard area. By this means, the pattern of ink-containing and non-ink-containing grid pixels of an OCR printed character is determined by sensing the pattern of voltages generated in the transducer array.

Various commercial devices (made by Recognition Equipment, Inc., and Siemens of Germany) in the form of hand-held wands (see Fig. 8.7) make use of arrays which have 9 transducers along the horizontal axis and 15 vertically. The ink/no-ink pattern can be applied to a ROM in a parallel mode, in contrast to the laser beam's serial mode, and recognition is accomplished at maximum speed.

The sensing surface of a transducer array can be projected by optical means onto any surface on which an OCR character might lie. In addition, this optical projection can be swept along any path over which an OCR message is composed. During such a linear sweep each character is sensed in turn at the instant a pattern of voltages, generated by the transducer array, conforms to one previously recorded in a ROM.

When applying the transducer array technique, the projected image must reproduce the area required by NRMA standards and its orientation must match that of the pixel grid. In other words, the image utilized in reading an OCR character must be both of standard size and accurately positioned, so as to precisely cover any printed character of interest. That is, the image must reproduce the standard area in terms of size, and its orientation must match the pixel-grid axis to the character axis within the required tolerances.

Figure 8.7. An OCR wand. Reproduced with permission of Caere Corporation.

The maximum skew difference between these two axes is commonly specified at $\pm 8°$. In addition, the projected image must be scanned along the line of a complete message by such means as to cover each character in sequence, according to the same rigid locational/orientational standards as was true for one character. Thus both image size and axis skew must be held constant (within close tolerances) in any method of NRMA–OCR scan.

When sensing with a two-dimensional transducer array, the area suspected of containing a printed message is flooded with light. As the transducer array is swept along a message path, it can be turned on and off in a sampling process not unlike that of taking a series of photographic snapshots. What the array sees in each such snapshot, as defined by its voltage pattern, is then compared to the ROM patterns. An identification is made whenever a particular snapshot achieves a match. One commercial device takes a snapshot every 300 micro-seconds.

With one commercially available hand-held wand (Caere Corporation), a linear array of transducers in the vertical direction develops one axis of the required pixel array, while the horizontal axis is established as the wand is swept across each character. Here the scan height (or vertical component of the scan path) is determined by some kind of scanning mechanism contained within the wand, while the horizontal component of the scan path is established in a manually driven wand sweep. In such an arrangement, the vertical component of the scan path is performed at constant speed over a fixed distance. But the horizontal component is variable in terms of both scan velocity and scan distance. Considering these variables, it is difficult to see how a linear array can ever hope to achieve the performance of an area array, since the decoding algorithms must take care of a number of different scan velocities, while a snapshot can subsist on any scan velocity below some maximum.

From the above discussion, it should be obvious that the greater the number of pixels in the search pattern, the better the chances of identifying one character as opposed to another. At the same time, more pixels imply longer scan times, more expensive arrays, and larger ROM capacities. Commercial practice at any given time compromises between identification capability and performance in terms of scan time and hardware cost.

VIDICON OR EQUIVALENT

While OCR messages can be beam-scanned under rigidly controlled conditions, OCR characters cannot be identified by existing algorithms if the scan height is varied simultaneously with the scan velocity. This of course precludes the reading of OCR characters by beam scan, where the distance between scan head and scanned surface is variable.

However, it is perfectly possible to project the image of an OCR message by optical means from any surface to the sensitized transducer array of a Vidicon or equivalent (TV camera) device. In one such instrument (Datacopy, Inc.), an entire area (which might include a complete message) is divided into a matrix with a "million" pixels. The presence or absence of ink (including some decision with the partially covered pixels) is transferred to a megabit memory, after which an analysis is performed on the information in memory. This technique can be used to read encoded messages of fairly great length and high complexity. (In fact, it is commonly used to verify the pictures on dollar bills.)

Where cost is of little interest, the Vidicon technique will read information projected from any distance and in any orientation. In fact, a Vidicon array is so extensive, the problem of partially covered pixels is of no material consequence.

ECONOMICS

It is now fairly obvious that OCR page readers are a fundamental part of the word-processing "explosion," and as such will ultimately be found in the front office of every organization in the world. It is therefore not unreasonable to ask: if OCR is here to stay in the technology of page readers, why should it not also be used in label reading, so that one technology is used throughout an organization? The answer lies in the fact that those variable factors which compromise OCR label reading (i.e., distance between scan head and scanned surface, skew, etc.) are constants in page readers.

In interpreting the above paragraphs, it should be remembered that the basic objective addressed here is that of automating the collection of transaction descriptions to the degree possible. The use of a hand-held device to read labels can hardly be called "automation." Unless a label can be beam-scanned from a distance under conditions where the label may be oriented in a direction random to the scan path the technology is not suitable for general factory-floor applications.

Almost any technological problem can be resolved by various means which extend over a spectrum from "elegant" to "heroic," where heroic implies very high cost. In this discussion, "heroic" applies to Vidicons and their equivalents, which are simply too expensive for general use. In comparing the relative "elegance" of the OCR and bar-code arts, consideration should be given to the following factors:

First, *cost*. Reading OCR is a two-dimensional process, as contrasted to bar codes and magnetic stripes, which are read in one dimension. Without doubt, it will always cost more to read OCR than bar codes. From a systems standpoint, this one issue becomes increasingly significant as data-collecting points move from work centers to work stations, so that many more data-collecting points are established.

Second, *signal quality*. The electric signals obtained from a scanning process oriented in two directions are continuously variable in terms of their magnitude, as contrasted to the on/off data obtained from a one-dimensional scan process. This variation imposes a strain on both the reading electronics and the decoding algorithm, which in turn limit both character set and reliable read performance.

Third, *read speed*. Because of a two-dimensional scan requirement, the linear movement of an OCR wand must be restricted in relation to what can be accomplished by a one-dimensional process. As a human tends to wand at a velocity of 10–30 inches per second, a human now reading with a hand-held OCR wand must remember to scan slowly.

Fouth, *skew*. The Y scan axis (or the vertical axis of a matrix grid), and the axes of the character to be read, must be codirectional within very narrow tolerances. Current state of the art is $\pm 8°$, while the near-term future tolerance is thought to be $\pm 10°$. This introduces a very real problem, since a human tends to sweep a hand-held wand in an arc. If the length of a message is relatively short—say seven to nine characters—it is fairly easy to maintain the necessary $\pm 8°$. However, when the message gets out to the 20 characters or so found in many factory-floor applications, manual wanding becomes a bit awkward, to say the least. Slot scanners or other skew-restricting means are often suggested as an answer to this problem. But these impose an unacceptable restriction on document formats.

Fifth, *rejection rate.* In reading OCR messages, each character must be identified and verified before it is worthwhile to pass on to the next character. As there is a rejection rate inherent to such a process, the longer the message, the less the read success. Current state of the art is a 1% per character rejection rate. With a 20-character message, the best that can be hoped for is an 80% first read rate.

Sixth, *automated reading.* OCR characters cannot be beam-scanned if the distance between a coded surface and a beam source is variable. That is, existing algorithms cannot handle variations in the Y direction simultaneous with those experienced in the X direction. This means that transaction description collections cannot be fully automated, if labeling is based on OCR characters, without using a Vidicon type approach.

Seventh, *substitution error rate.* The information contained in OCR characters is not very redundant. (What redundancy is available is different from bar-code redundancy.) With OCR it is possible to obscure a portion of a character and still tell what that character is. But this portion is not very great with most characters. In fact real problems are encountered in discriminating between *1* and *7, 4* and *9,* and even *5* and *6.* Because of low redundancy, the potential substitution error rate for OCR is more than 100 times higher than for CODE–39. In fact, substitution error rates as high as one in 10,000 are quoted for some hand-held wands, while OCR page readers are no better than one in 30,000. In contrast, CODE–39 has at least the potential of one in 1,000,000 or more.

The National Retail Merchants Association has standardized OCR for machine-readable labels used in collecting point-of-sale transaction descriptions. The banks similarly have settled on MICR, while the grocery stores are now stuck with the UPC bar code. While all three of these technologies are demonstrably inferior to 3/9 or 2/5 discrete bar codes, they are without question embedded in the system and are not now subject to change. Any vendor hoping to sell products in this market must work with the embedded codes, whether they are optimum or not.

By no means does this mean that any of the above should be considered for use in factory-floor applications. Figures 8.3 and 8.4 list the alleged advantages and disadvantages of OCR in the factory environment. While some of these may be open to argument or even differences of opinion, the bottom line is simple: the bar-code art is much more read-reliable and format-flexible, and significantly less expensive to read, than any OCR labeling technique.

Just as OCR can never hope to compete with appropriately constructed bar codes, neither can the magnetic stripe technology, albeit for different reasons. The next chapter examines these reasons.

9. Magnetic-Stripe Technology

While there are many variations on a basic theme, magnetic-stripe recording is not really all that different from printing bar codes. In magnetic materials there is a two-state choice of polarity, just as there is a two-state choice between either black or white in many printing processes. In fact, with magnetic recording there are "fences" of plus "pickets" structured against minus backgrounds (or vice versa), analogous to black bars on white backgrounds. In both circumstances information is delineated by the locations on recording media where there are either plus/minus flux or black/white color changes.

Just as with bar codes, information is recovered from magnetic stripes by sweeping read heads across entire coded surfaces and converting positional information into pulse-width modulated voltages. (See the encoder/reader in Fig. 9.1.) As recovered voltages are exactly the same in both circumstances, there is no inherent first read rate or substitution error rate difference between the two technologies. Rather, these issues are functions of how well particular vendors design their instruments and what patterns of pickets they elect to use.

On the other hand, because magnetic materials are more homogeneous than most printing materials, information can be packed more densely on magnetic stripes than bar codes can be printed on conventional papers. While these higher packing densities are advantageous in some circumstances, they require the use of smaller wand tips. Rubbing on abrasive magnetic materials, these smaller wand tips will not last as long as the larger tip jewels used on some bar-code wands.

The sensing elements currently found inside magnetic wand tips have been designed around a number of different magnetic phenomena including the Hall Effect, the Magnetostrictive/Piezoelectric Effect, magnetic transistors, and one of the several magneto-resistances. At the present time, magneto-

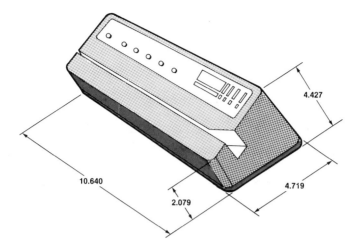

Figure 9.1. An encoder/reader.

resistors appear to be simpler and less expensive than the alternatives and are most commonly used. In this application, magneto-resistors have a depth of field of about 0.007 inch. This means, that for all practical purposes, wand tips must be held in contact with magnetic stripes during read traverses. Or at best, the magnetic stripes can be covered only with a very thin film of non-magnetic material.

As the coding density potential for magnetic stripes is superior to that of bar codes, magnetic stripes may well have an advantage in those applications where a great deal of information must be machine-read from data cards. Then too, where information stored on a card is subject to change (to up-dating), the magnetic stripe technique may well be the only practical answer. But these attributes have limited application to general manufacturing problems, and other traits inherent to magnetic recording are limiting. For instance, it is difficult to print magnetic stripe labels. Certainly the use of adhesive magnetic-stripe labels manually attached to multiple copies of documents is not a pragmatic solution to document identification systems. Further, magnetic stripes cannot be read from a distance, data destruction of magnetically encoded messages is not visible if it occurs, magnetic stripes cannot be made an integral part of many products, and magnetic stripes can easily be erased by an imposed magnetic field of very few gauss. (For a summary of the advantages and disadvantages of magnetic stripe reading, see Figs. 9.2 and 9.3.)

MAGNETIC STRIPE READING

- DISADVANTAGES
  - EXPENSIVE MEDIA
  - NOT HUMAN READABLE
  - MODIFIABLE
  - WORD PROCESSING INCOMPATIBLE
  - DIFFICULT TO COPY
  - RESTRICTED FORMAT
  - LOW PRINT RATE
  - CANNOT BE READ THROUGH PLASTIC COVER
  - NOT BEAM SCANNABLE

Figure 9.2.

MAGNETIC STRIPE READING

- ADVANTAGES
  - READ-WRITE CAPABILITY
  - LOW ERROR RATE
  - NON-CRITICAL WANDING
  - FULL CHARACTER SET

Figure 9.3.

MAGNETIC-STRIPE TRAVELER

As already noted, a *traveler* is one documentary means of communication between a centralized Production Control organization and a large number of individuals operating in widely dispersed work stations. Here communication is two-way: Production Control directs, while operators report progress and problems.

Travelers are typically batched in large numbers at central locations from which they flow out to many work stations. To be effective, a traveler should provide space for a considerable number of human-readable characters, so that Production Control can articulate its intentions in adequate detail. But in addition, a traveler should provide some control over the means by which performance is reported back to Production Control. In other words, a well-crafted traveler's format includes both human-readable text and appropriate preorganized machine-readable messages.

In the past, the hole-punched hollerith card was widely used as a traveler. Here the information carried in the punched hole pattern can be machine read. However, because of its limited capacity—only 80 human-readable characters and 80 ciphered equivalents—such a document is useful only as a skin sheet to otherwise supplied information. This falls far short of the sophistication required by today's Production Control.

IBM introduced the magnetic-stripe card concept (see Fig. 9.4) for use as a traveler to replace the hollerith card. This was done for several reasons, including:

- The magnetic-stripe technology was perceived as offering maximized read reliability of the enciphered data in the rugged environments experienced on many a factory floor.
- Magnetic-stripe slot readers are probably the least complex, lowest-cost, and most reliable device which can be used to read machine-enciphered information of any kind. Such a reader is tough and inexpensive, and requires practically no maintenance.
- Magnetic-stripe cards offer space for 700 alphanumeric, human-readable characters (ten lines of text, each line seven inches long, with a packing density of ten alphanumeric characters per inch.)

Unfortunately, IBM's engineers were carried away by their concept of magnetic stripes to be located anywhere and read by hand-held wands. As a result, they compromised the potential of the magnetic stripe by restricting its packing density well below that which is possible for slot readers. This was

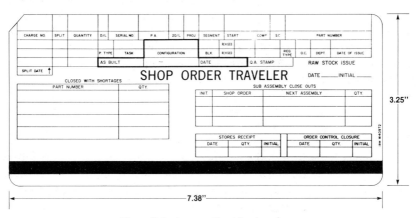

Figure 9.4. A magnetic-stripe traveler.

necessary, because the sensitized tip of a wand must be protected against wear and other damage by a cover whose thickness lifts the transductive element above the surface of the magnetized medium. As the depth of field which extends above this surface decreases with increased packing density, that density must be limited to the point where the depth of field still extends through the cover to the transductive element located inside the wand's tip. (Fig. 9.8 shows Track 1 and Track 3 enciphered with a much higher density than Track 2. They can be read only with slot readers, while Track 2 can be read by either slot readers or hand-held wands.)

The potential use of hand-held wands limits the machine-readable text to 70 ciphers (one line of text seven inches long, with a packing density of ten alphanumeric ciphers per inch). Here ground is lost because the hollerith card offers 80 ciphers! Further, IBM salesmen suggest that information in the magnetic stripe be repeated several times in order to maximize the chances of a read—in order to have a high first read rate.

By the time all the above issues are considered, there is little room left in a magnetic stripe for information other than a job order number or its equivalent. This means that, when transaction descriptions are collected, only the job order number is read automatically; the other parts of the descriptions must be introduced manually through the use of a keyboard.

While the technology was compromised (in terms of packing potential) for the benefit of the hand-held wand, a wand, as compared to a slot reader, is a fragile device. Wands do not stand up well in the typical factory environment and some companies, committed to magnetic-stripe travelers, will allow only slot readers out on their factory floors.

The pros and cons of the magnetic-stripe card technology may be argued indefinitely. But the very rigid format, and the limit to its machine-readable information, precludes the use of such a card as a general-purpose traveler. As shown by Figure 9.5, the magnetic-stripe traveler concept can be expanded to provide a set of detailed instructions. However, it should be noted that the format required by these instructions precludes the use of a magnetic-slot reader. Therefore, anyone adopting the magnetic-stripe technology for general use is forced to live with the inherent shortcomings of hand-held magnetic wands.

MOVE TICKET

Travelers are batched in large numbers at central locations. The cost of a traveler printer is relatively unimportant as there is only one—or very few—in any system. *Move tickets,* on the other hand, are floor documents (see Fig. 9.6); it must be possible to print these, on demand, at many locations distributed over the production area. Since magnetic-stripe card en-

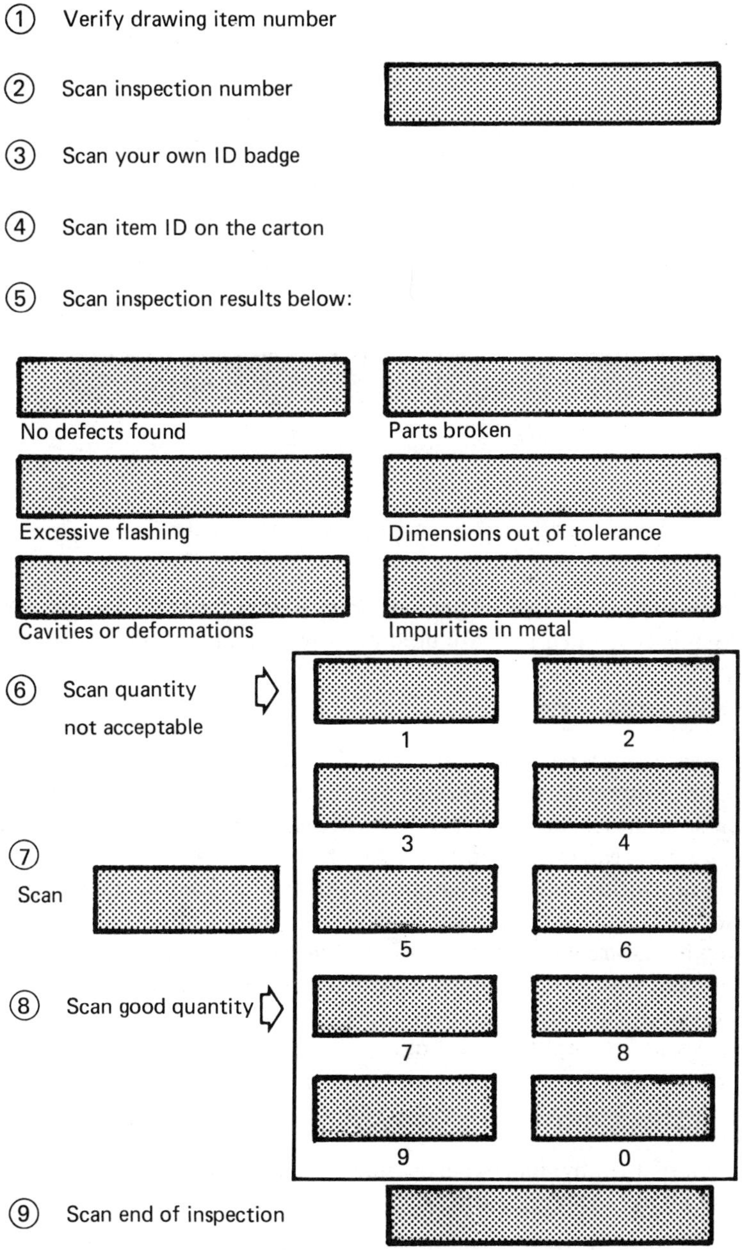

①   Verify drawing item number

②   Scan inspection number

③   Scan your own ID badge

④   Scan item ID on the carton

⑤   Scan inspection results below:

No defects found   Parts broken

Excessive flashing   Dimensions out of tolerance

Cavities or deformations   Impurities in metal

⑥   Scan quantity
         not acceptable

      1   2

      3   4

⑦
Scan   5   6

⑧   Scan good quantity
      7   8

      9   0

⑨   Scan end of inspection

Figure 9.5. A magnetic-stripe instruction sheet.

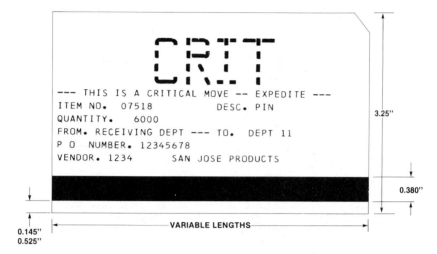

Figure 9.6. A magnetic-stripe move ticket.

coder/printers are fairly expensive units of hardware, it is very hard to justify this cost when they are used only in a demand mode.

TRANSPARENT COVER

Documents of interest are burdened by human-readable as well as machine-readable requirements. Although much is made of an ability to read magnetic stripes through layers of dirt, grease, or paint, this is of small value if the human-readables are obscured. When documents are exposed to contaminating influences, it is common practice to enclose them in plastic envelopes. If such an envelope is transparent, and if an appropriate choice of reading hardware has been made, both human- and machine-readable data can be read through the cover. But magnetic-stripe documents cannot be read through such a cover; they must be removed from their protecting envelopes to accomplish a reading.

SECURE ID CARD

The right of an individual to participate in a transaction requires the machine identification of three factors:

- Something carried: a unique key, card, etc.
- Something known: a password (unique or common), etc.
- A physical attribute: a voice print, fingerprint, hand profile, picture, etc.

All current ID cards have limited machine-readable capacity which can provide only unique identification numbers. While descriptions of the other factors might be held in a central memory and called forth at the time of a transaction by the identification number, this is not logistically practical in many circumstances.

If an individual is to participate in an off-line secure transaction, as is commonly the requirement, he must carry a card which provides more than an identification number. Such a card must provide a machine-readable description of a physical attribute and space for a password, as well as a unique ID number. This calls for kilobits of memory. Further, an appropriate card must be of such a technology that each user can code the card in any way deemed desirable, in a process down-loaded from a conventional digital computer's archive memory.

It is generally conceded, by many who have considered the problem, that such a card must be based on a fusible-link PROM. However, at the present time at least, there is no such card available. At the same time there is very strong pressure to improve the security of transactions, while making do with currently available technologies.

In response to this pressure, the industry has coined the buzz phrase "secure ID card." Nobody is quite sure what this term means in an absolute sense, but relatively speaking it references some kind of card which is more secure than an ID card bearing its unique number in a pattern of hole perforations. Perforated cards have several useful characteristics: they are rugged, easy to machine-read, and very easy to fabricate. Unfortunately, they are also easy to copy. Once copied, the illegitimate copies freely par-

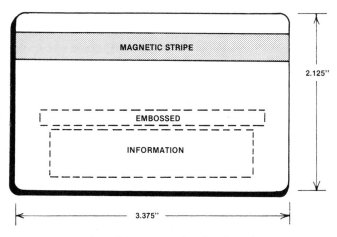

Figure 9.7. A magnetic-stripe ID card.

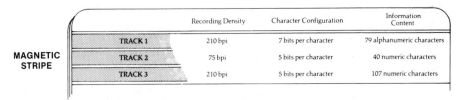

	Recording Density	Character Configuration	Information Content
TRACK 1	210 bpi	7 bits per character	79 alphanumeric characters
TRACK 2	75 bpi	5 bits per character	40 numeric characters
TRACK 3	210 bpi	5 bits per character	107 numeric characters

Figure 9.8. A magnetic-stripe ID card: format.

ticipate in unauthorized transactions, so that the originals' basic purpose has been made irrelevant.

In its search for more security, the industry has decided that magnetic-stripe cards are "secure" (see Fig. 9.7). How it reached this conclusion is difficult to see. In Mr. J. R. Scantlin's well-publicized contest, Cal Tech students are alleged to have come up with 22 different ways of copying the information encoded into magnetic stripes.

3M Corporation has helped the situation somewhat by offering their "high coercivity magnetic-stripes." This material can only be coded—or erased—by special magnetic heads which are capable of generating the required strong magnetic fields. While this does offer better security for the time being, it is a temporary measure at best, for any magnetic material which will accept coding can be erased and re-encoded by someone who has taken the trouble to find out how it is done. So while the high coercivity stripes may be "foolproof," they are not "sailor proof"!

Figure 9.8 indicates three magnetic-stripe card formats as these are established by the American National Standards Institute (ANSI).

10. Integration

The movement whereby discrete manufacturing transactions are increasingly supported by bar-coded messages represents a relatively small portion of a very broad general-information-processing evolution. The basic objective of this evolution is to collect pertinent information by means which are automated to the degree possible. As a consequence, all production control decisions should be considered in terms of how they relate to other components of a rapidly expanding mosaic of what heretofore have been considered separate and diverse applications. Within this mosaic, interrelationships are now expected. A particular application which uses one bar-coding scheme must now be evaluated in terms of how it performs when exposed to systems utilizing OCR, magnetic-stripe, or other bar-code schemes.

WORD PROCESSING

There is a rapidly increasing demand for word-processing systems wherein the words are supplied from computerized archives. This demand has created a tremendous market for typewriter type printers which can function as computer peripherals. The market response to this demand includes both horizontal and vertical mechanical dot-matrix machines as well as devices operating on daisy wheel, ink-jet, thermal, electrostatic, and other principles.

Just as these printers have created a tremendous explosion in the amount of paper generated by some computer centers, so must this returning rain of documents be digested in other offices also oriented toward computer technology. Here the market response includes a number of page scanners based on OCR technology. In this sense, OCR readers provide the means for returning the printed text to computer memory. By combining printers and OCR, the automated write/read cycle can be continued indefinitely.

This paper torrent relates directly to manufacturing processes, because each sheet passing through a manufacturing transaction represents an item whose identification must be integrated with the identification of all other items. If each printed sheet is individually identified by a combined bar-code/OCR- header, sheet identification can be accomplished by the same instruments used to identify any other item passing through the system. In fact, if such a header is adopted as a printed page standard, bar-code readers can function as the most cost-effective means of item identification throughout one fully integrated organization: office correspondence, engineering drawings, purchase documents, and manufacturing records.

While daisy wheel printers cannot normally print bar codes in the desired configurations, other printer technologies are available to accomplish this goal. Using any matrix printer with a graphics capability, a header (or label) can be bar-coded while the text is written in an OCR font. The central office can then use its page readers on the text, while the outlying stations pick up the header with inexpensive bar-code reading instruments.

Label reading and documentary text recovery are two completely different tasks which should not be confused. The objectives of text recovery are not unlike those of retrieving information from any other memory form. The fact that OCR may go well with page reading, or that magnetic stripes provide a useful means of storing information on data cards, has little to do with how pages or data cards are labeled.

Automated item identification is the issue addressed by this discussion. This should be based on the use of inexpensive labeling techniques. There is no rational reason why the tasks of labeling and label reading should be burdened by the technical restrictions and higher cost of either OCR or magnetic-stripe technologies. As OCR and bar codes are print-compatible and can easily be fused into one system (while magnetic stripe is a foreign technology), a decision to use both human-readable characters and bar ciphers in a labeling scheme is both pragmatic and economic.

MAGNETIC STRIPE

As a result of extensive sales efforts, primarily by IBM, many MIS systems are now based on magnetic-stripe documents. This situation is a bit ironic, for magnetic stripes perform many functions very well indeed. In fact, magnetic slot readers are the toughest, most indestructible, and longest lasting maintenance-free devices imaginable for operation in the hostile environments of the typical factory floor. Unfortunately, magnetic stripes simply cannot perform many of the tasks now expected of general-purpose document networks. Therefore, sooner or later, organizations now using magnetic-stripe documents will have to bite the bullet and regroup around bar codes. Sad—but these are the facts of life.

The magnetic-stripe ID card offers an even tougher proposition. As long as financial institutions stick with this technology, corporate security organizations may well lean in the same direction. As Corporate Security is seldom concerned with production efficiency, Production Control often faces a fait accompli when it comes to the ID card they must use. While bar codes offer better security than do magnetic stripes, neither is very good; those organizations interested in real security will focus on chip-in-card techniques. One answer, used by many organizations, is to add a bar-code label to each ID card, without worrying much about what else is on or in those cards.

OTHER BAR CODES

During the bar-code evolution, those promoting each new application have tended to add their own unique code. Here the basic human urge to create has reached undreamed-of heights, and the situation is a mess: CODE-11 for ATT vendors, CODE-39 for Department of Defense vendors, UPC for U.S. point of sale, EAN for European point of sale, CODABAR for the U.S. Blood Bank, and so on.

So far, the efforts of each standardizing committee have focused on only one application. As a result, their conclusions cannot be applied to other applications. Even with basics such as point of sale, equipment worldwide must address the UPC, EAN, and JAN codes. In fact, even these have versions to take care of special situations. Several organizations are facing this problem by developing a "tier" algorithm which can discriminate between certain codes and then decode the chosen code. Some are developing a "chip" for UPC, EAN, and JAN, while others are considering one chip for both CODE-39 and I-2/5-CODE. Much of this effort has the implications of the "rubber glove" business. (There once was a manufacturer of leaky fountain pens who added rubber gloves to the product line so customers would not stain their fingers!)

While it is difficult to predict how this evolution will progress, it is evident that CODE-39 is the only general-purpose bar code now in common use. Without much doubt, CODE-39 will survive through future evolutionary steps. The same cannot be said for any other bar code.

OTHER SYSTEMS

One focus of the bar-code art makes practical the automation of certain processes. Here, to be effective, it is often necessary to combine both printing and reading instruments, along with process machinery, into completely integrated systems. Even now labeled tote boxes, in queue on carousel, are kicked off into available work stations under the prerogative of Production Control. Further, automated warehouses issue bar-coded routing labels with their pick lists. Delivery to the indicated destination is assured merely by slapping one of these labels onto each item before tossing it on a conveyor. Figure 10.1 shows one application of bar-code tracking on an automated conveyor where each item is uniquely identified at an automated weigh station.

But some processes are not satisfied with only type designators and routing information. For instance, in the meat-packing industry, each container is further characterized by its unique weight. This weight is established on the fly at an in-line weigh station. As shown in Figure 10.2, an applicator located down stream from the weigh station affixes a label indicating both individual weight and a unique license number. It is the license number, addressing an archived memory, which is used to prepare shipping manifests and billing documents.

Figure 10.1. A weigh system. Reproduced with permission of Accu-Sort Systems, Inc.

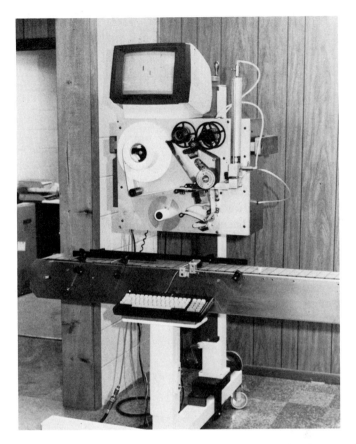

Figure 10.2. A label application system. Reproduced with permission of York Tape and Label Corporation.

STANDARDS

As listed in Appendix E, more than a dozen different organizations are now trying to control standards for applications in which they have vested interests. Unfortunately, most of these cannot agree among themselves on what is appropriate in terms either of coding scheme or print format. While CODE-39 has become the main industrial standard, it is not universally adopted at this time.

The Uniform Container Standard of Figure 10.3 (not using CODE-39),

Figure 10.3. Uniform container standard.

could be merged into MIL-STD-1189, along with the automobile industry standard, to give one standard which could be used by all where the only difference between one label and some other would be in their message lengths.

The TIER-CODE has been suggested as a universal standard suitable for all applications.

11. Conclusions

In the recent past, bar coding was regarded simply as a technique which made it possible for instruments to read labels. As such, it was commonly compared with perceived alternatives such as MICR, OCR, and magnetic stripe. But now bar coding is the generally accepted means of documenting information using a machine language. Within this expanded concept, there is no economic alternative to bar codes. Bar coding provides the only straightforward method of printing bit-streams—byte-configured series of ones and zeros. As this is the logic around which all digital computers are organized, there is nothing tricky or devious about using bar-coded messages to communicate with digital computers: bar-codese is a computer language. The concept is basic and will not be replaced by some "other" technique in a few years; it is here to stay.

Just as printed documents function as a basic means of communication between human minds, so bar-coded documents can link widely distributed instruments of diverse kinds into inexpensive, flexible, highly reliable paper-communication networks. In short, bar coding is a network technique.

As more and more individuals absorbed the possibilities, 1981 and 1982 saw a tremendous movement to bar coding throughout the discrete manufacturing community. Tool control, quality control, material control, field service applications, and the like all received attention. Of most importance, however, bar coding has rapidly become the cornerstone of many MRP programs.

Those concerned with improving the effectiveness of Production Control were originally attracted to bar coding because it gives a central authority a very tight grip over the way performance is reported from many widely distributed work stations. But interest quickened when it was realized that, through the use of bar codes, document sophistication can offset hardware costs. That is, in many circumstances an interactive wand, working with appropriately designed documents, can be used in lieu of a terminal.

Further, the manual controls on almost any electronic instrument can be replaced by a single receptacle into which a bar-code wand is inserted when its services are required. Such instruments are adjusted, as desired, in response to printed bar-code instruction sets. The implications here are revolutionary: instruments of every kind—field, process control, laboratory, etc.—will ultimately be redesigned to capitalize on this feature. This will happen because, by this means, it is possible to feature greater versatility at lower cost, coupled with superior environmental tolerance and less maintenance—an unbeatable combination. With this technique, documents can be used to direct work as well as report progress.

The network concept is gathering momentum in applications beyond the manufacturing milieu. In their ZPS system, the German TV industry plans to characterize/time-stamp every program with a 32-bit interframe message: month, day, hour, minute, station, country of origin, and type of program. This same information is then bar-coded in their *TV Guide* for use in programming video recorders. Both Texas Instruments and Western Publishing bar-code talking books, while Casio bar-codes music and Hewlett-Packard bar-codes computer programs. Now software "smiths" can look forward to a reduction in the tedium of key transference, when word-processing instruments automatically print programs both in their familiar form and in the bar-code equivalent. And just think how the wrong-number rate will be reduced when telephone directories are bar-coded! All these applications expand the network concept.

MARKET CONFUSION

Unfortunately, this pervasive movement is now inhibited by four issues: (1) the confusion engendered by the proliferation of bar-coding schemes; (2) the fact that those bar-code features which determine both print and read reliability are not well understood; (3) the performance characteristics of available printers; and (4) the lack of inexpensive reading devices which do not require manual manipulation. (As regards the last point, bar codes are commonly read either by laser scanners which are quite expensive, or by wands which must be moved by hand; neither technique is appropriate in many situations.)

However, the near-term introduction of electrostatic printers will make possible higher quality printing, while simple linear array readers (such as those based on CCDs) will provide reasonably priced automated scan. It is the purpose of this handbook to illuminate the other issues, so that anyone who wishes to implement a bar-code system will understand what he is about and can be assured that his system's performance will be optimum.

Bar coding involves four completely independent but interrelated, processes: (1) printing; (2) transforming from space (what is printed) to time;

(3) use of an algorithm to decode the time phase; and (4) a coding scheme which facilitates all the other processes. Existing commercial devices introduce major variables into each of these four processes. As a result, the performance of current bar-code systems are unnecessarily diverse, and the full potential of bar coding is not achieved. This disorder is a direct result of the fractured nature of the bar-code market as now constituted. A number of small organizations set the tone as they attempt to sell their hardware and to promote those bar-coding schemes which they have concocted as a means of proprietorizing their hardware. There are literally dozens of "house codes" offered, most of which include more or less irrational features directed to one objective. Many of these features compromise performance in general applications.

DISCRETE/CONTINUOUS CODES

Bar-coding schemes may be either discrete, where each cipher ends with a bar, or continuous, where each cipher ends with a space. A number of continuous codes are now in common use, but all of these are restrictive.

Ciphers of a discrete bar code can be treated as just another font, as far as printing processes are concerned. That is, discrete bar codes can be printed by conventional typewriters (at least those with large type), rubber-belt stamps, or any other printing process which depends on individually movable type. Such processes are relatively inexpensive when applied to bar-code printing.

Continuous codes cannot be printed in this way. Here a complete message must be composed as one unit and printed in one pass. Under these restrictions, film masters are commonly prepared, one for each label. While this is not a serious cost, if one film master is used to print hundreds of labels, it imposes an oppressive burden on randomly printed messages. While the I-2/5-CODE has generated a lot of interest because of its cipher-density potential, its use in general circumstances is a mistake: there are many applications in which its printing cost is much higher than that of a numeric-only discrete code.

The UPC-CODE is a continuous code of fixed length and may be so regarded by an algorithm. On the other hand, the use of any continuous code (such as Paper-Byte or I-2/5-CODE) is subject to character dropouts when used in systems which mix messages of various lengths. Even UPC applications would be better served with a discrete cipher set.

In short, discrete codes offer maximum readability and maximum printability to the point where continuous codes should never be used in any circumstance!

COLOR OF SCAN LIGHT

Many solid-state devices—lasers, light-emitting diodes (the LEDs used in hand-held wands), even light-sensitive transducers—work most effectively with infrared light, generally above 900 nanometers in wavelength. At the same time, humans—and the printing inks to which humans best respond—function in the visible portion of the light spectrum: 400 to 700 nanometers.

Unfortunately, most commonly used inks are blind to infrared. That is, many inks observed by the human eye cannot be seen by an infrared scanner. Therefore, if an infrared scanner is to be used, bar-coded messages must be printed with a special ink, generally a carbon ink. Since carbon inks respond over the whole range—from below 400 to above 900 nanometers—why isn't their use a rather neat solution to this whole problem?

First, at the present time at least, carbon inks are not as stable physically as are the more popular inks. They cause a lot of niggling problems—smears, wear on print mechanisms, and the like—which can add up to a lot of money in logistic costs. But the main economic issue lies in the logistic cost of putting bar-coded messages on any item—packages, documents, etc. If the machine-readable label is to be printed with a special ink, every item must be processed twice: once for the text, art work, etc., and a second time for the label. The need for double processing will cost industry a tremendous amount of money—all of which is completely unnecessary.

By far the best answer to the color issue is to specify all system components—inks, scan lights, transducers, etc.—as to their performance at 700 nanometers (visible red). The use of carbon ink or other special inks should be forgotten. All programs should be capable of working with both those inks now commonly in use and those which will shortly be in use. Granted, earlier hand-held wands did work with a minimized signal/noise ratio when designed for infrared, but that was in the past. Present technology makes it just as easy to design suitable hardware for 700 nanometers or thereabouts (HeNe lases at 633 nm).

In fact, systems trying to use scanning devices which operate only in the infrared portion of the spectrum will not be able to capitalize on some of the coming printer innovations. Many of these are directed to a performance in respect to human eye response. These include ink-jet, thermal-ribbon, and electrostatic printers; printing inks which are capable of standing high temperature; inks which diffuse into substrates to give very reliable long-lived labels; or other special applications.

PERFORMANCE EXPECTATIONS

All of this leads to the question: What kind of performance can be expected using existing hardware—mechanical printers and hand-held wands? The answer is: Quite good. On the other hand, a quantified answer is almost impossible to postulate, because it depends both on how well wands and printers are maintained, and on the degree to which their idiosyncratic functions are understood by their operators.

Today's print/wand technologies suggest that if one uses USD–3—printed on a white or red background with blue or black ink, with a check cipher included in each message—a first read rate of better than 80%, with a substitution error rate of less than one in one million, can be maintained economically in an extensive facility where documents are printed on diverse printers in different coding densities, and where these documents are read at hundreds of different locations with hand-held wands in various states of wear. Because of multiple scans, the first read rate issue becomes moot when either laser or linear array scan techniques are used. At the same time, the use of a check cipher in each message to minimize the substitution error rate remains important, no matter what scanning technique is used.

All discrete manufacturing organizations will be forced to go with bar coding sooner or later. There simply is no other way of maximizing the effectiveness of Production Control. Bar-coded messages significantly tighten communications between Production Control and each operator in his work station and minimize the cost of such communications, while bar-coded labels make it possible for anyone to know where everything is. For this one application, at least, the confusion engendered by the broad choice of codes is stripped away: USD–3 can be used without concern that someday it will be replaced by some other code. (The Tier concept expands on USD–3 but does not replace it.) Hopefully, the Department of Defense will drop its infrared

Figure 11.1. The past is prologue. Reproduced with permission of SCAN Newsletter.

scan requirement because of associated high costs and application restrictions. But only those organizations dealing with the Department need to concern themselves with the infrared problems.

While existing hardware—particularly wands and printers—leaves much to be desired in terms of performance, it can be used successfully now. The introduction of new devices will doubtless improve system performance, but will not otherwise change the way a system functions. Regardless of what hardware is used, the success of any program will depend on a detailed understanding of those factors which effect performance, a thorough training of operating personnel, and careful hardware maintenance.

Bar coding is now clearly identified as the only cost-effective means of printing a machine language. As such, applications will continue to proliferate. The past is certainly prologue! Who knows what new chick will crack forth from the bar-code egg?

Appendix A
Bar-Code System Issues

The issue addressed here is that of automating the collection of transaction descriptions quantified in terms of the classical WHAT, WHERE, WHEN, HOW, WHO, and WHY.

In the discrete manufacturing milieu, an *operation* is commonly considered to be a basic WHAT-UNIT. But this particular increment is always associated with other what-units of both smaller and larger size. The tree-up, from a coordinated series of operations, represents a work unit identified by a job order number. Treeing down from the same point are those items involved in the completion of an operation: material, parts, packages, tools, etc., *and* the documents used to drive the various processes. At the very least, every operation is described by two transactions: START and COMPLETE (unless it can be assumed that, once started, a completion inevitably follows).

From this logic, it should be obvious that every item passing through each transaction must be identified by a machine-readable label if transaction description collections are to be automated. From this opportunity has sprung a labeling/label-reading community supplying material, preprinted forms, printers, and readers. As applications have proliferated, members of this community have developed their own proprietary house codes in order to sell their products. As long as individual applications were well separated from other applications, the use of an individual house code was no particular problem. Now, as these applications merge into a mosaic of interaction, the lack of coding standards is restraining the market.

It is increasingly apparent that bar coding is a technology whose applications far exceed those of simple labeling. Bar coding represents a basic means of communication with computer-oriented systems used at the local (work-station) level as an alternative to keyboards. Machine-readable bar-coded instructions are now used to automate the direction of action as well as to identify items.

In many applications which can be addressed with this technology, it must be possible to print extensive bar-coded messages anywhere on a page as desired, and to mix these messages in with human-readable text with complete flexibility. Machine-readable message objectives include maximum cipher set, maximum coding density, and maximum read reliability. As it is not possible to achieve all these goals simultaneously, some form of code compromise may be expected. It is, of course, the force of compromise which has led to the development of so many different house codes.

Unfortunately, the bar-code art is now confused, and its read reliability compromised, through the efforts of all vendors as they market their particular products and promote the bar-coding schemes supported by these product lines. As a result, no bar-coding scheme now in common use has the assured read reliability of which the art is capable. In fact, discrete bar codes with minimum cipher set utilizing four coding components, where the wide components (bars and spaces) are at least three times the width of the narrow components, offer maximized read reliability under the worst conditions—the widest latitude of print quality and of hand-wanding velocity variations.

Considering all ramifications, CODE-39, printed with a 3/1 component width ratio and restricted to 39 ciphers (USD-2), offers the maximum read reliability when an alphanumeric cipher set is required. The 3/9-CODE, which is really a superset of CODE-39, offers 80 ciphers (½ASCII), although with some loss of read reliability because of the expanded cipher set. On the other hand, CODE-B, a subset of CODE-39, gives maximum read reliability by limiting algorithmic choice to a purely numeric cipher set.

Because of these relationships, all three of these codes can be read by the same firmware. And as long as the START/STOP ciphers are unique for each coding scheme, these three codes can be mixed in one system without compromising the features of any one code. Further, as bar codes which use 3/1 component width ratios can be printed with narrower bars and spaces than can any code based on a 2/1 ratio, only I-2/5-CODE can be printed in higher density than can CODE-39 with alphanumerics, or CODE-B where numeric-only will do the job. Schedule A.1, "Relative Print Density of Various Bar Codes," illustrates this point.

In short, this "multideck" or tier bar-coding scheme combines maximum read reliability with maximum density while still allowing an 80-character cipher set. Further, it achieves all these objectives without compromising the standards now being set by the Department of Defense, the automobile industry, and others. To use it, all that is required is the rewriting of firmware.

BAR-CODE SYSTEMS DESIGN

The bar-code art is based on a number of different coding schemes which variously address the issues of (1) printing; (2) transforming what has been printed into electronically composed information; and (3) interpreting the derived information in its electronic form. All these systems are organized around the binary-number concept, whereby a particular portion of an encodement represents either a one or a zero.

Information is maintained originally in the space domain, as printed. An area which might possibly contain a printed message is arbitrarily divided into segments, each of which is assigned meaning depending on whether or not it is covered by ink. (The presence or absence of information, at a point in space, is established by the presence or absence of ink.) This spatially organized pattern can be transformed into an electronic signal either as a space-intact pattern (by Vidicon, Reticon, or swept

Schedule A.1. Relative print density of various bar codes.

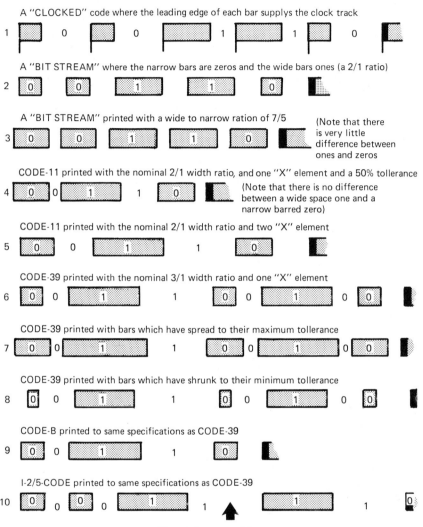

A "CLOCKED" code where the leading edge of each bar supplys the clock track

A "BIT STREAM" where the narrow bars are zeros and the wide bars ones (a 2/1 ratio)

A "BIT STREAM" printed with a wide to narrow ration of 7/5   (Note that there is very little difference between ones and zeros

CODE-11 printed with the nominal 2/1 width ratio, and one "X" element and a 50% tolerance   (Note that there is no difference between a wide space one and a narrow barred zero)

CODE-11 printed with the nominal 2/1 width ratio and two "X" element

CODE-39 printed with the nominal 3/1 width ratio and one "X" element

CODE-39 printed with bars which have spread to their maximum tollerance

CODE-39 printed with bars which have shrunk to their minimum tollerance

CODE-B printed to same specifications as CODE-39

I-2/5-CODE printed to same specifications as CODE-39

The minimum possible space in which the byte "00110" can be printed.

linear array) or by converting from space domain to time domain by swept light beam (hand-held wand or laser scan). Further, a particular coding scheme can be considered at both bit and byte levels. Some systems are interested in identifying only a particular unique byte from some finite number of pre-established bytes, while others are concerned with bit-streams of any format and any length.

CODING COMPONENT SCHEMES

It is possible to consider any bar-coded message as a stream of elemental bits—both ones and zeros—which might occur in any conceivable order. It is fairly easy to tell the difference between the ones and the zeros, but in the absence of clock signals it is very difficult to separate individual ones (or individual zeros) from a string of several ones (or zeros) which might occur together in sequence, one following the other.

Therefore in bit-oriented systems where information is to be presented as a stream of ones and zeros, combinations of elemental ones and elemental zeros are assigned "one" and "zero" significance. Each such assigned bit is constructed as a simple elemental pattern of both bars and spaces. By these means, each individual bit (bar and space) can be identified by the transitions from bar to space and space to bar without reference to clock signals. (In Schedule A.2, coding component schemes A, B, and C are used in various bit-oriented systems.)

Some bar-coded messages are further divided into a series of individual bytes where each byte represents a particular member of a family of associated bytes. Under these circumstances the family association is established by features which are common to every byte, while individual bytes are identified by features unique to a particular byte.

Schedule A.2. Coding component schemes.

Definitions:

Elemental "bit" = Eb	Narrowest possible bar width (X) = "1"
	Narrowest possible space width (X) = "0"
Assigned "bit" = Ab	Arbitrary combination of "Ebs," to form a "Nybble"
Component	Arbitrary combination of "Abs," to form a "Byte"

A. *Fixed-Interval Bar/Space Ratios* (bit-oriented)
This technique utilizes two coding components wherein both have the same width (i.e., the same number of Ebs).

Wide bar/narrow space   Eb = 110   Ab = 1
Narrow bar/wide space   Eb = 100   Ab = 0

B. *Variable-Interval Bar Ratio* (bit-oriented)
This technique utilizes two coding components with different widths.

Wide bar/narrow space   Eb = 110   Ab = 1
Narrow bar/narrow space   Eb = 10   Ab = 0

C. *Bar Duoratio Interleaved with Space Duoratio* (bit/byte-oriented)
This technique utilizes two coding components wherein the widths have either a 2/1 or 3/1 ratio.

Narrow bar		Eb = 1	Ab = 0
Wide bar	Eb = 111,	Eb = 11	Ab = 1
Narrow space		Eb = 0	Ab = 0
Wide space	Eb = 000,	Eb = 00	Ab = 1

D. Interleaved Quaternary Bar/Space (byte-oriented)
This technique utilizes four coding components wherein the widths have either a 2/1 ratio or 3/1 ratio.

Narrow bar		Eb = 1	Ab = 1
Wide bar	Eb = 111,	Eb = 11	Ab = 11
Narrow space		Eb = 0	Ab = 0
Wide space	Eb = 000,	Eb = 00	Ab = 00

E. Bar Multiratio Interleaved with Space Multiratio (byte-oriented)
This technique can utilize up to eight coding components wherein the widths have 2/1, 3/1, and 4/1 ratios.

Eb = 0	Ab = 0	Eb = 1	Ab = 1
Eb = 00	Ab = 00	Eb = 11	Ab = 11
Eb = 000	Ab = 000	Eb = 111	Ab = 111
Eb = 0000	Ab = 0000	Eb = 1111	Ab = 1111

Parity:		Count:	
	Elemental zeros		Elemental bits
	Elemental ones		Bars
	Assigned zeros		Spaces
	Assigned ones		Wide bars
	Bars		Wide spaces
	Spaces		Components
			Wide components

The unique features used to identify a particular byte are the various combinations of wide or narrow bars or spaces which can be achieved without violating any family relationships. (In Schedule A.2, coding component schemes C, D, and E are used in various byte-oriented systems.) Bytes are integrated into complete messages (or words) either as discrete increments which may be identified individually (stand alone), or as continuous bit-streams which must be sorted out by the reading electronics.

Comparisons of the structures of various bar-coding schemes are shown in Schedule A.3.

CODE INTERPRETATION

Bar coding involves three completely separate processes: printing what is intended (within width tolerances); transforming from space mode (as printed) to time mode by swept light spot (within sweep-velocity tolerances); and interpreting the time mode by algorithmic analysis.

The raw material with which an algorithm works is limited to the detection of transitions from high to low voltage and from low to high voltage. By some means, the algorithm must determine the relative times at which such transitions occur. This is accomplished by using a high-frequency pulse train, commonly called "clock pulses,

Schedule A.3. Comparison chart for some popular bar codes.

CODE	TYPE CODE	CODE components	CIPHER set	CIPHER elements + space	CIPHER components	WIDTH RATIO Wide/Narrow bars & spaces	PATTERN bar space	PATTERN wide/narrow
TELEPEN	C	4	128 ASCII	16	vary	3/1	none	none
TELEPEN Double density	C	4	29	16/2	vary	3/1	none	none
CODE-128	C	8	102	11	6	2,3,4/1	BSBSBS	none
CODE-128 Double density	C	8	13	11/2	3	2,3,4/1	BSBSBS/2	none
CODE-39 Printed 3/1	D	4	43	16	9	3/1	BSBSBSBSB	2/5 bars 1/4 spcs
CODE-39 Restricted	D	4	39	16	9	3/1	BSBSBSBSB	2/5 bars 1/4 spcs
3/9-CODE	D	4	80 ½ASCII	16	9	3/1	BSBSBSBSB	3/9 cmpnts.
CODE-B	D	4	10	10	5	3/1	BSBSB	2/5 cmpnts.
CODABAR	D	4	24	12–14	7	3/1	BSBSBSB	2/7,3/7 cmpnts.
MSI-CODE	C	4	10	12	8	2/1	BSBSBSBS	4/8 cmpnts.
I-2/5-CODE	C	4	10	9	5	3/1	$B_SB_SB_SB_SB_S$	2/5
CODE-11	D	5	11	8	5	2,3/1 bars 2/1 spaces	BSBSB	1/5 or 2/5
UPC	C	8	10	7	4	2,3,4/1	BSBS	none
2/5	D	2	10	14	5	3/1	BBBBB	2/5

PARITY		STREAM LENGTH	MESSAGE OVERHEAD	LENGTH (NUMERIC) UPC	"XXXX"	
bit / zeros & ones	component / bar & space	bits	ciphers START/STOP check & cipher set	equivalent	full element	half element
none	none	vary	3or4	207	111	56
none	none	vary	4	143	95	48
1-e 0-o	b-3 s-3	vary	3	142	76	no
1-e 0-o	b-3 s-3	vary	3	87	54	no
1–9 0–6	b-5 s-4	15	2or3	207	111	56
1–9 0–6	b-5 s-4	15	2or3	207	111	56
1-o 0-e	b-5 s-4	15	2or3	207	111	56
1-o 0-e	b-3 s-2	9	2or3	139	59	30 *minimum discrete*
1-e 0-o	b-4 s-3	11–13	4	181	77	39
none none	b-4 s-4	12	2	151	55	no
1-e 0-e	b-5 s-5	vary	2or3	117	45	23 *minimum*
none	b-3 s-2	7	3	105	55	no
1/0-e 0/1-o	none	42	4	95	N/A	N/A
1-o 0-e	b-5	13	3	181	97	46

as a time base. This "clock" is not the same as the clock track used to indicate the presence of ones and zeros. These clock pulses must occur fast enough to divide time into increments much smaller than those represented by a minimum print component, either bar or space.

A key issue in algorithmic performance is an ability to measure pulse widths (analogous to both bar widths and space widths). This is accomplished by using voltage transitions to gate clock pulses into counters. The counts accumulated in a number of counters are then compared, and the pulse-width pattern is deduced from this comparison.

Algorithms address pulse-width modulated voltages which are supposed to represent an analog of the print intention. This analog may, of course, be faulty to the degree allowed by the tolerances of both print width and sweep velocity.

Bar/space widths are established as relationships—one bar to another, or one space to another—by the ratio of counts accumulated in two counters. Assuming constant sweep velocity, it matters little either what sweep velocity is used or in what cipher density a coded message is printed. Width ratio is the issue of significance. Further, considering a four-component code, it is necessary only to tell the difference between wide and narrow bars (between low-high and high-low transitions) and between wide and narrow spaces (between high-low and low-high transitions). It is not necessary to decide between wide bars and narrow spaces, or vice versa.

In most circumstances of printing, it can be assumed that all bar-width tolerances will be on either the high or the low side. The circumstances would be unusual indeed if some bars were wider than nominal, and others were on the narrow side. Therefore, in an appropriately designed algorithm, relevant ratios can be established as long as a minimum bar or space is still large enough to be detected—as long as the minimum bar or space is at least equal to one print element.

Sweep velocity, on the other hand, may well be highly variable within the sweep of one message. When a human uses a hand-held wand, there is a tendency to start slow, speed up in the middle, and end slow. Under these circumstances, measurements made between bar widths in the middle and those of either end can easily get into trouble. However, with a discrete code—depending on the algorithm used—it may only be necessary to measure bar-width ratios within the confines of one cipher; a wider tolerance on the sweep velocity can be accepted by the system.

A general rule for bar coding is: for messages carrying more or less the same amount of information, more simple ciphers are read more reliably than fewer complex ciphers. CODE-39 has 43 possibilities constructed from combinations of 15 bits, while CODE-B has only ten ciphers constructed by using nine bits. Under these circumstances, four CODE-B ciphers (representing 6,561 possibilities) can be read with more assurance than can two CODE-39 ciphers (1,849 possibilities). This is true even when two CODE-39 ciphers consume only 32 bits, while four CODE-B ciphers take 40 to do the same job.

BAR/SPACE WIDTH VARIATIONS

When a printing process is used to print a line on a printable medium, the printed line will have a width which is different from that of the printer line. This width difference depends on the printing process, the ink used in that process, and the characteristics of the printable medium. In almost any printing process, then, the printer line is caused to grow in the process of forming the printed line.

Line growths do not increase line widths by some percentage; rather, they add given increments regardless of line widths. That is, the narrower the line, the greater the percentage change imposed by line growth. Line growths are not constants; their nominal values carry tolerances. For example, one particular letterpress job showed a line growth of 0.005 inch ± 0.003 inch. Here, if the printer line is 0.008 inch wide, the printed line would have a nominal value of 0.013 inch but would actually vary in width from 0.010 to 0.016 inch or 0.013 inch ± 23 percent.

Each printing process is subject to its own unique line-growth pattern. In fact, if any factor in a process is changed (ink, medium, etc.), both the line growth and its tolerances may be expected to change. Here the general effect of a changed variable is to increase the tolerances over those which might otherwise be expected in a consistent process.

This problem is particularly serious with mechanical dot-matrix printers, where process variables are in a constant state of flux. Assume, for instance, a line marked by a hammer blow through an inked ribbon. Here two process variables require consideration. First, the amount of ink forced from the ribbon by a given hammer blow is quite different, depending on whether the ribbon is new or used. Second, the amount of ink forced from a ribbon depends on the characteristics of the hammer strike, which in turn is a function of hammer deceleration. Not only do hammer decelerations have their own tolerances to consider, but their operating points tend to wander over the life of each adjustment.

Further, in mechanical dot-matrix printers, a print hammer is scanned back and forth over the surface of a recording medium. Because of this lateral movement, a dot printed from such a hammer is slightly displaced in the direction of a hammer scan. If two adjacent dots are scanned from opposite directions, their displacement will be oppositely directed. Part of this displacement is a consequence of lost motion in the scan mechanism, but part is also a function of medium texture: the softer the medium, the greater the displacement. The bar printed to the right of Figure 7.4 illustrates this phenomenon.

TOLERANCE IMPLICATIONS

There are two basic bar-width coding assumptions in common use: one where discrimination between lines whose nominal widths are "X" and "2X" is presumed possible, and one where this is not possible and detectability is based on width ratios of at least 3/1. If 2/1 is possible, eight different coding components can be used: "X," "2X," "3X," and "4X" wide bars, and "X," "2X," "3X," and "4X" wide spaces. (Here it is assumed that the greater the number of different coding components used, the higher the code density possible.)

On the other hand, if 2/1 is not practical and 3/1 must be used, only four coding components are possible: "X" and "3X" wide bars, and "X" and "3X" wide spaces. (In this case it is assumed that the narrower the width of the coding components possible, the higher the code density which can be achieved.)

In composing bar codes from wide and narrow bars or spaces, the wider the wides in relation to the narrows, the easier it is to tell the difference between a wide and a narrow. It may therefore be assumed that a code which uses wide bars or spaces which are three times the width of its narrow bars or spaces is more read-reliable than is one which uses a 2/1 ratio.

The issues addressed here include an inclination to print at the highest possible density; a desire to achieve the maximum read reliability; and the acceptance of a particular width tolerance under which a line "X" wide (the narrowest possible bar or space) can be printed.

In printing bar codes at their highest possible density, the wide bars or spaces must have widths which are integral multiples of "X." If this were not so, a higher density would be possible. If the tolerance on the width of "X" is ± 50%, it is not possible to tell the difference between a wide "X" and a narrow "2X." On the other hand, it *is* possible to tell the difference between a wide "X" and a narrow "3X." To tell the difference between one bar and another twice as wide, the tolerance on the bar must be less than ± 25%. Therefore the width of the minimum bar or space which can be used in an eight-component code is twice as wide as one which is based on four components.

Considering lost motion in the print head's scanning movement, dimensional changes over ribbon life, shifting print-head adjustments, and sidewise skid of the hammer blow, a ± 50% tolerance on "X" (which in this case is the hammer diameter) is the best that one could hope for with any mechanical dot-matrix printer. So it can only be concluded that four-component bar-coding schemes are most practical when bar-coded messages are to be printed with mechanical dot-matrix printers at maximum density.

CODING OVERHEAD

All bar-coded messages must include some ciphers which are not relevant to the information carried by that message, but which are required for housekeeping purposes. At the very least, there must be START and STOP ciphers, which are used to supply the decoding algorithm with certain essential bits of information. First, they establish the presence of a message. Second, they establish the direction of scan. Third, they can be used to develop a general feeling (rhythm) for the rate of scan. Further, in those circumstances of constant velocity scan (as in beam scan), they can give some indication of print-width tolerance (ink spread).

There is a tendency for the more complex cipher sets to use longer START/STOP codes. For instance, TELEPEN uses 1010101010111000 (16 elements) for START, while CODE-39 calls on 100010111011101 (15 elements) for both START and STOP. On the other hand, CODE-B (a compact, discrete, numeric code) uses only nine elements for both START and STOP.

(*Note:* In printing bar-code patterns in this text, a one is used to show the position of a bar while a zero shows the position of a space. By underlining all the ones, it is then possible to envision the pattern of printed bars which will result when the underlined portions are extended vertically into full-length bars.)

In a numeric-only situation with few numbers in the message, and where message length is a major issue, it is hard to justify a complex, lengthy START/STOP situation even where (as in the circumstance of TELEPEN and CODE-128) double-density enciphering is possible. In other words, the overhead on TELEPEN and CODE-128 (or CODE-39 for that matter) is very high for short, numeric-only messages.

Another overhead issue is the potential value of a modulo (check-sum or "message parity") check cipher. Here the value of a check cipher depends on whether the code is continuous or discrete. Discrete codes are potentially more secure than continuous codes, particularly continuous codes where the message length is variable.

The issue here lies with the partitioning of the bit-stream. In a discrete code, each cipher represents an individually partitioned bit-stream which can be evaluated as a stand-alone proposition. For instance, each cipher of CODE-39 is composed of 15 bits in some kind of characteristic stream which can be examined and acted upon without concern for any other portion of the bit-stream. In a continuous code, on the other hand, the entire bit-stream must be analyzed as one long "glob."

In general, the maximum read security (the minimum substitution error rate) is always achieved through the use of a check cipher. However, the value of the function performed by this cipher is less in a discrete code than in a continuous code, and the shorter the message, the less the value in discrete codes.

Several codes make it possible to use one cipher set to represent more than one character set. The UPC and TELEPEN include a "system" cipher in their overhead, while CODE-128 accomplishes the same objective by using a choice of START ciphers. This technique is commonly used to determine whether the bulk of the message is coded alphanumeric or double-density numeric—or even some other character set.

CIPHER DENSITY

Bar-code specifications are not generally intrinsic. Rather, they are derived from the performance of particular printers. Here, the derivation includes such parameters as a minimum printing element (bar or space), width tolerance, maximum cipher density, even print-contrast ratio.

As one example, the specifications for CODE-39, as established by Intermec, Inc., are written around the serial impact printer offered as a part of that company's product line. Here the minimum print element of 0.0075 inch happens to be what is printed when that particular machine is used with a dry carbon ribbon. When CODE-39 is printed on a Printronix printer, the hammer size and the characteristics of ink-impregnating fabric ribbon establish the minimum print element at 0.020 inch, nominal. Here the width tolerances are a function of ribbon life. Both these machines leave much to be desired in terms of print quality, print-contrast ratio, and bar-width tolerances.

With the advent of electrostatic printers, laser and other, the potential for print quality is vastly improved, and as a result, all codes can be printed at high density. In addition, the print-contrast ratio can be maintained consistently above 85% where the read reliability is maximized. Certainly, with these instruments a minimum print element of 0.005 inch is easily achieved with a width tolerance of better than ± 10 percent. This gives a reliable cipher density for CODE-39 of 12/inch (28 ciphers in 2½ inches!). Electrostatic printers are capable of printing in higher densities, but given the environment experienced on the factory floor, a 0.005 inch print element may be as small as one would wish to go. Higher resolutions are increasingly susceptible to post-printing contamination.

Many of the issues discussed here stem directly from a desire to print in the highest possible density, in order to keep a bar-coded message as short as possible. Minimizing the area required for printing messages is one objective. But in addition, a barcode message should be less than three inches long if it is to be read by hand-held wands. While the UPC minimum print element is 0.010 inch wide, the message length is restricted to 12 ciphers. Considering part numbers, possibly concatenated with work-order numbers, the factory environment calls for messages which are on the average at least twice as long as those of UPC design. Under these circumstances a print element of one half the width is consistent with a message which must be twice as long.

As electrostatic printers achieve more usage, bar-code read reliability should improve. This is true because the mechanical printers now in use, and the printing process used for UPC, must strain to meet their print specifications, and a fair percentage of printed labels now fall outside these limits. Electrostatic printing, in contrast, is much more uniform in terms of both print contrast and dimensional accuracy.

ALGORITHMIC DECISIONS

The word "algorithm" describes a mathematical process whereby a conclusion is reached by following a series of logical, preestablished propositions, each of which in regularized sequence calls for a decision—a choice between various possibilities. From this concept may be deduced the fact that the fewer the number of choice possibilities encountered at each step of the sequence, and the easier it is to choose, the more reliable the process.

In the first place, in composing bar codes from wide and narrow components, the wider the wide components in relation to the narrow components, the easier it is to tell the difference between a wide and a narrow. Therefore a code which uses wide components three times the width of its narrow components is more reliable than one which uses a 2/1 ratio. (4/1 is even more reliable.)

In fact, the fewer the different kinds of coding components used, the more reliable the coding system. The 2/5-CODE uses only two bar widths; CODE-B, I-2/5-CODE, and TELEPEN use two bar widths and two space widths; CODE-11 uses three bar widths and two space widths; while the UPC and CODE-128 use four different bar widths and four different space widths.

Discrete codes (those ending in a bar) are more reliable than continuous codes (those ending in a space), because each cipher of a discrete code can be evaluated as a separate entity, while ciphers must be reconstructed from complete messages when using continuous codes. And of course, the smaller the cipher set, the more reliable the coding system. Numeric-only codes require only one choice in ten; alphanumeric, one choice in 36; ½ ASCII, one choice in 56; while full ASCII requires one choice out of 128 possibilities.

When interpreting the bar code of a particular cipher, an algorithm might first establish the legitimacy of that cipher as an accepted member of a predefined family of ciphers. Once the family pattern is assured, then the decision can be made which determines which member of the family is represented. Family characteristics might include: a standard pattern of bars and spaces; a standard pattern of wide and narrow components; bar/space parity; standard length of bit-stream; bit parity; and actual counts instead of parity. As an example, the restricted CODE-39 always has two wide bars out of five bars, and one wide space out of four spaces. This leads to a fairly secure code. On the other hand, CODABAR might have 1/4 bars and 1/3 bars and 1/3 spaces, *or* 2/4 bars and 3 spaces, *or* 1/4 bars and 1/4 spaces, which must be considered a weak code because the family characteristics are not tied down. Considering all these issues, CODE-B proves to be the most secure code possible.

In spite of the above complex rhetoric, one might well ask if it is at all significant. As a matter of fact, it can easily be shown that it is possible to read any unique cipher with or without family relationships. The answer lies with the read variables—print qualities, cipher densities, scan-spot sizes, scan velocities, optical and electrical noise, and the like—which will be encountered in the real world. The greater the variables faced, the greater the need for code security. However, if a particular system works to satisfaction, why knock it?

CLOCKED CODE

Moving information formatted in the binary number system, by relating the presence or absence of a pulse in one circuit to the presence of a clock pulse in a second circuit, is common industry practice. Here the presence of a pulse in an information circuit, which occurs at the same time as a clock-pulse, represents a binary one. The absence of an information pulse at a clock time represents a binary zero.

As shown by Figure A.1, it is possible to duplicate this format by printing both an information track and a clock track. With such a scheme, both tracks must be read simultaneously. As this cannot be accomplished conveniently with hand-held wands, scanning laser beams, or any other linear scan system, the concept has little merit when compared to the alternatives.

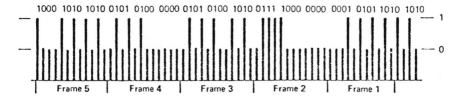

Figure A.1. A clocked code.

TIER-CODE

The point of departure for any coding scheme would be best served by the USD-2 code as specified by the Materials Handling Institute, Inc.—if only they had specified a 3/1 ratio for the wide/narrow components. This code has the tightest possible structure (2/5 × 1/4-CODE) which provides a full alphanumeric character set plus "space", ".", and "-". It is unfortunate that one cipher was wasted by its use as START/STOP, and that one the inverse of the P cipher.

However, the world seems to be focusing on CODE-39 as *the* standard. Certainly it is *the only general-purpose code* now in common use, all other codes being special-purpose codes which are in some way compromised for general use. CODE-39 is a very good code, but it is not as strong as its USD-2 subset because it includes four ciphers which do not conform to the 2/5 × 1/4 pattern of USD-2. Because CODE-39 is a trade mark of Interface Mechanisms, this code is commonly called the 3/9-CODE. But this is patently inaccurate because the 3/9-CODE offers 80 ciphers, while CODE-39 boasts only forty-three. The use of the 3/9 designation for CODE-39 adds further confusion to the bar-code scene. CODE-39 is better called USD-3, if trade marks are an issue.

The focus on USD-3 leaves two problems. One is the cipher-set restriction, and the other is the real estate consumed when a numeric system will suffice. Acres of real estate are saved by dropping two bars and two spaces to reach CODE-B. At the same time, the addition of a narrow space and a narrow bar to USD-2 has the potential of much more than full ASCII. In short, a multitier structure (CODE-B numeric, USD-2 alphanumeric, 3/9-CODE-½ASCII, and USD-2 plus bar and space full ASCII) is the optimum general-purpose structure. Here the whole structure can be treated as one code. An appropriate algorithm will first decide which tier is being read and will then take advantage of all the features offered by each individual tier.

This is a print-forgiving system which utilizes all safeguards, avoids the limitations inherent to all continuous codes, and is consistent with MIL-STD-1189. With this plan, one reading system can read labels printed in any one of the tier levels as these are mixed at random. By these means, one system maximizes performance in every conceivable application; no other code is needed.

One semiconductor chip can then be designed for this algorithm which will serve inexpensively in all circumstances. That is, any tier—or any mixture of tiers—can be used independently, and any reader (wand, linear array, or laser beam) can read the result with maximum read reliability under the worst print conditions. The wide components should be three times the width of the narrow components within a tolerance of ± 25% the width of the narrow components, where the narrow bars are the same width as the narrow spaces within the same tolerance, and the print contrast at 700 nanometers is held to better than 85%. A given printer could then print in whatever density was possible, consistent with these specifications. (This can meet MIL-STD-1189's three densities, if that is desired.) However, if the minimum elemental width is 0.005 inch, as it can easily be with electrostatic printers, the CODE-B tier is printed in a density of at least 20 ciphers per inch.

At the same time, where a lower level of read reliability is acceptable, the wide components should be three times the width of the narrow components within a tolerance of ± 50% of the narrow width, with the narrow bars the same width as the narrow spaces within the same tolerance, and the print contrast at 700 nanometers held to better than 55%. With these specifications, mechanical dot-matrix printers can be used. The use of two sets of print specifications underlines the effects of print quality on read reliability.

FIRST READ RATE

It is almost impossible to quantify the performance of wands and printers, because such performance depends on how well they are maintained and the degree to which their idiosyncratic functions are understood by their operators. Many of the published performance claims are ludicrous. For instance, bar codes by themselves do not "perform" as claimed in much of the literature; only complete systems perform. The decoding algorithm is every bit as important as the coding scheme used.

While any salesman worth his salt can prove that his products meet their published specifications, this is only possible as long as they are in tiptop shape and manipulated by skilled operators in friendly environments. Such demonstrations are not entirely relevant. A perhaps equally valid test would draw on the services of documents printed on out-of-adjustment printers, using either new or badly worn ribbons, where readings are attempted using worn wands held at preposterous angles.

Obviously, the real world lies somewhere in between these two extremes.

BAR CODE PROGRAM

- MANUAL WAND
- LASER SCANNER
- BEAM SCANNER
- PORTABLE TERMINAL
- PERSONAL TERMINAL
- SATELLITE WAND ADAPTER

- PAGE PRINTER
- TICKET PRINTER
- LASER PRINTER
- HEADER PRINTER
- LOGGER

Figure A.2. Bar-code program.

Appendix B
Bar-Coding Schemes

The first success achieved by bar coding was in applications where labels were printed off-line in batches, using fairly high-quality printing processes. Here, automating the collection of point-of-sale transaction descriptions, particularly in the grocery business, has produced several fairly happy years of field experience. Most of the organizations involved do not use a printer of any kind, being concerned only with reading bar codes.

Interface Mechanisms, Inc., was an early pioneer in applications which required on-site printing of labels using information drawn at random from computer archives. Their serial impact printer more or less became *the* industry standard where a very small document (2″ × 4″ or less) of severely restricted format could do the job. Many applications are now based on the availability of inexpensive page printers with a full graphics capability by which bar-coded messages in any format can be placed on a page in any orientation and at any location.

At present, mechanical dot-matrix printers of various configurations are being used to print bar-coded messages. While these can be made to function, their performance leaves much to be desired: this technology can never print bar codes which can be read with maximum reliability. This is true because such printers cannot be made to print continuously with high quality (uniform in dimension and uniform in print contrast) and at high density. Inevitably, with any "damp" ribbon printer, print characteristics change significantly with ribbon life.

Sooner or later, electrostatic and thermal ribbon printers will replace mechanical printers of all kinds, where bar coding is an issue, because the newer technologies have the potential of turning out high-quality documents at a continuous rate. In fact, laser printers are now available from several organizations, which do print in high quality, but at a high hardware cost. For the time being, then, mechanical dot-matrix printers will have to suffice, until inexpensive electrostatic or thermal ribbon printers reach the market.

The bar-code art has grown like Topsy in many directions to the point where literally dozens of codes have been proposed (see Figure B.1). Many of those suggested address the issue of how to print at the highest possible density using a particular printing process. Many of these codes were developed at a time when the objectives of bar coding were not well understood; as a result, they have little if any merit today.

Figure B.1. Bar-coding schemes. Reproduced with permission of Creative Data Services, Inc.

However, a number of these, regardless of merit, are embedded in the system and are not going to go away or be replaced by a "better" code, no matter how much better that code may be. The UPC code is fixed in the grocery business for purposes of point of sale; doubtless it will remain. Similarly, the EAN code of Europe will continue to perform there.

CODABAR is now a de facto standard with the Blood Bank and other health care organizations; perhaps it will remain. Whether the MSI code, used in inventory control, has enough vested interest to fight off competition may be in question. Certainly neither CODABAR nor the MSI code are "strong" codes in terms of the criteria discussed in this handbook. TELEPEN in Europe and CODE-128 in the United States may both survive, but their applications will be limited. The full ASCII character set is not a general requirement and the price paid (in terms of reduced read reliability and higher hardware costs) is too high for general use. CODE-39—constrained as discussed elsewhere—is both theoretically and practically the most reliable code possible for full alphanumeric messages. The weight of support from the Department of Defense and the automobile industry should carry it through to an industry standard without much trouble.

Because   CODE-39 takes up so much space, however, a numeric-only higher density code is required for a fall-back position. At the present time, some feel this should be the I-2/5-CODE, because this code can be printed in the highest possible density, while others opt for CODE-11. However, I-2/5 is limited in its applications because it is a continuous code, while CODE-11's read reliability is less than optimum because of the coding components used. When these deficiencies become recognized, attention might turn to CODE-B because this is, theoretically as well as practically, the most read-reliable code, and it can be printed in the highest possible density of any discrete code.

Whatever develops, it is increasingly apparent that most bar-code reading (and printing) instruments will be required to address at least two different bar codes distributed at random throughout one system. (MSI faces this problem now; their instruments read both the MSI and the UPC codes.)

Another consideration in this shake-out of many special "house" codes to a few industry standards is the fact that, as applications spread, various codes collide head-on. For instance, the UPC code is used successfully in point-of-sale transactions with the grocery trade. From here it has migrated to point of sale for auto parts. At the same time, as the UPC code cannot be used in factory-floor applications, CODE-39 will be used by Production Control in the auto industry. Sooner or later each auto part will have its own part number (probably embossed on the part), wherever CODE-39 is used. When this happens, does it make sense at the point of sale to have every part carry messages encoded with two different schemes?

Be that as it may, the issue may ultimately be decided by the performance of the hand-held wand which can be sold at the lowest possible price. As the lowest cost is achieved when the light source, light detector, and decoding logic are all integrated onto one semiconductor chip, whoever designs such a chip will set the stage for standardization around the decoding logic used. At the present time, Hewlett-Packard seems to be the only company in the United States with both a commitment to wand design, and a chip-design capacity. Perhaps their efforts will have the final say.

UPC*

The logic of the UPC bar-coding scheme is based on the premise that the width of any line printed on paper (by gravure, letterpress, or flexography) will have a tolerance of as much as ± 0.003 inch. The logic further concludes that it is possible to tell the difference between a narrow line and one which is supposed to be twice as wide, if the tolerance on the narrow line's width is no more than ± 24% and that of the wider line ± 12 percent. The basic element (line or space) of the UPC bar code is, then, 0.013 inch; a given minimum line or minimum space may have a width anywhere between 0.010 and 0.016 inch (24% of 0.013″ = 0.003″).

With these modular constraints, the UPC coding logic utilizes bars and spaces whose widths are one, two, three, or four times the width of the basic element—eight different coding elements (see Fig. B.2). A UPC coded message is represented by a bit-stream where an elemental space is assumed to be a zero and an elemental bar a one. As there can be no clock track (to identify the presence or absence of a bit) in this bar-coding scheme, it is necessary to create a pattern from which the bit-stream can be deduced by other means. This is accomplished by forming every UPC cipher from two bars and two spaces, where each bar/space combination is some integral (1, 2, 3, or 4) multiple of the elemental width 0.013 inch, where the total number of elements used is always seven, and where all ciphers either start with a zero and end with a one, or vice versa (see Schedule B.1). These requirements limit the bar-space combinations to the point where they will only support a numeric designating system of ten possible combinations.

Other features of the UPC code address the need that it should be very easy to read a coded message correctly, but very hard to read it incorrectly. (The first read rate should be high, while the substitution error rate should be low.) Thus the format is limited to 12 ciphers divided into two halves of six ciphers each (two streams of 42 bits), where the right-hand stream has odd parity and the left-hand even parity, and where a modulo-check cipher is incorporated into the right-hand stream. In addition

Figure B.2. The Universal Product Code.

*Uniform Product Code Council, Inc.

Schedule B.1. The UPC cipher set: ten ciphers.

First Character Set	Left Cipher	Right Cipher
0	0001101	1110010
1	0011001	1100110
2	0010011	1101100
3	0111101	1000010
4	0100011	1011100
5	0110001	1001110
6	0101111	1010000
7	0111011	1000100
8	0110111	1001000
9	0001011	1110100
	START & STOP	101
	CENTER	01010

7 elements/cipher
12 ciphers in standard message
95 elements in standard message (7 × 12 + 2 × 3 + 5)

the left-hand cipher, in the left-hand stream, is used to designate which of a number of possible character sets is represented by the other ciphers.

Once the above assumptions are tied down, the density of the UPC can be adjusted to the width tolerance actually experienced under a particular set of circumstances: if a width tolerance of less than ± 0.003 inch is possible, the cipher can be printed with coding elements which are less than 0.013 inch.

From beginning to end, the UPC code is continuous: that is, the spaces between ciphers are a part of the code.

CODE-128™*

It is possible to consider CODE-128 as if it were an adapted superset of the UPC coding scheme. This code achieves 102 possible combinations by expanding the UPC's seven elements to 11 and the UPC's two bars and two spaces to three bars and three spaces.

Because of the greater number of read choices (102 versus 10) which must be made by the decoding algorithm, and the much longer variable-length bit-streams possible (limited to 42 bits in the UPC), the potential read reliability, in terms of first read rate and substitution error rate, cannot be considered up to UPC performance. In addition, because CODE-128 utilizes eight coding elements, it cannot be printed on mechanical dot-matrix printers in high density. The ± 24% elemental tolerance re-

*Trademark of Computer Identics, Inc. Concept of T. C. Williams.

quired when using eight coding components cannot be maintained reliably with this printing technology at densities which are possible with other codes.

CODE-128 is organized so that it is possible to choose one of three different character sets which may be represented by the 102 ciphers (see Schedules B.2, B.3, B.4). This is done by using three different start-code choices where a particular start code indicates which character set is used in encoding the bulk of the message.

CODE-128 is continuous: the spaces between ciphers are a part of the code.

Schedule B.2.   CODE-128: cipher set A.

SP	11011001100	F	10001100010
!	11001101100	G	11010001000
"	11001100110	H	11000101000
#	10010011000	I	11000100010
$	10010001100	J	10110111000
%	10001001100	K	10110001110
&	10011001000	L	10001101110
'	10011000100	M	10111011000
(	10001100100	N	10111000110
)	11001001000	O	10001110110
*	11001000100	P	11101110110
+	11000100100	Q	11010001110
,	10110011100	R	11000101110
—	10011011100	S	11011101000
.	10011001110	T	11011100010
/	10111001100	U	11011101110
0	10011101100	V	11101011000
1	10011100110	W	11101000110
2	11001110010	X	11100010110
3	11001011100	Y	11101101000
4	11001001110	Z	11101100010
5	11011100100	[	11100011010
6	11001110100	\	11101111010
7	11101101110	]	11001000010
8	11101001100	⌢	11110001010
9	11100101100	—	10100110000
:	11100100110	NUL	10100001100
;	11101100100	SOH	10010110000
<	11100110100	STX	10010000110
=	11100110010	ETX	10000101100
>	11011011000	EOT	10000100110
?	11011000110	ENQ	10110010000
@	11000110110	ACK	10110000100
A	10100011000	BEL	10011010000
B	10001011000	BS	10011000010
C	10001000110	HT	10000110100
D	10110001000	LF	10000110010
E	10001101000	VT	11000010010

FF	11001010000	ESC	11110110110
CR	11110111010	FS	10101111000
SO	11000010100	GS	10100011110
SI	10001111010	RS	10001011110
DLE	10100111100	US	10111101000
DC1	10010111100	FNC3	10111100010
DC2	10010011110	FNC2	11110101000
DC3	10111100100	SHIFT	11110100010
DC4	10011110100	CODE C	10111011110
NAK	10011110010	CODE B	10111101110
SYN	11110100100	FUNC 4	11101011110
ETB	11110010100	FNC 1	11110101110
CAN	11110010010	STOP	1100011101011
EM	11011011110		Used for Table A
SUB	11011110110		START 11010000100

Schedule B.3. CODE-128: cipher set B.

SP	11011001100	?	11011000110
!	11001101100	@	11000110110
"	11001100110	A	10100011000
#	10010011000	B	10001011000
$	10010001100	C	10001000110
%	10001001100	D	10110001000
&	10011001000	E	10001101000
'	10011000100	F	10001100010
(	10001100100	G	11010001000
)	11001001000	H	11000101000
*	11001000100	I	11000100010
+	11000100100	J	10110111000
,	10110011100	K	10110001110
—	10011011100	L	10001101110
.	10011001110	M	10111011000
/	10111001100	N	10111000110
0	10011101100	O	10001110110
1	10011100110	P	11101110110
2	11001110010	Q	11010001110
3	11001011100	R	11000101110
4	11001001110	S	11011101000
5	11011100100	T	11011100010
6	11001110100	U	11011101110
7	11101101110	V	11101011000
8	11101001100	W	11101000110
9	11100101100	X	11100010110
:	11100100110	Y	11101101000
;	11101100100	Z	11101100010
<	11100110100	[	11100011010
=	11100110010	\	11101111010
>	11011011000	]	11001000010

(*Continued*)

Schedule B.3. (*Cont.*)

ˆ˙	11110001010	t	10011110100
—	10100110000	u	10011110010
\	10100001100	v	11110100100
a	10010110000	w	11110010100
b	10010000110	x	11110010010
c	10000101100	y	11011011110
d	10000100110	z	11011110110
e	10110010000	{	11110110110
f	10110000100	|	10101111000
g	10011010000	}	10100011110
h	10011000010	~	10001011110
i	10000110100	DEL	10111101000
j	10000110010	FNC3	10111100010
k	11000010010	FNC2	11110101000
l	11001010000	Shift	11110100010
m	11110111010	Code C	10111011110
n	11000010100	FUNC 4	10111101110
o	10001111010	Code A	11101011110
p	10100111100	FNC 1	11110101110
q	10010111100	STOP	1100011101011
r	10010011110		Used for Table B
s	10111100100		START 11010010000

Schedule B.4.   Code–128: cipher set C.

00	11011001100	22	11001110100
01	11001101100	23	11101101110
02	11001100110	24	11101001100
03	10010011000	25	11100101100
04	10010001100	26	11100100110
05	10001001100	27	11101100100
06	10011001000	28	11100110100
07	10011000100	29	11100110010
08	10001100100	30	11011011000
09	11001001000	31	11011000110
10	11001000100	32	11000110110
11	11000100100	33	10100011000
12	10110011100	34	10001011000
13	10011011100	35	10001000110
14	10011001110	36	10110001000
15	10111001100	37	10001101000
16	10011101100	38	10001100010
17	10011100110	39	11010001000
18	11001110010	40	11000101000
19	11001011100	41	11000100010
20	11001001110	42	10110111000
21	11011100100	43	10110001110

44	10001101110		75	11000010010
45	10111011000		76	11001010000
46	10111000110		77	11110111010
47	10001110110		78	11000010100
48	11101110110		79	10001111010
49	11010001110		80	10100111100
50	11000101110		81	10010111100
51	11011101000		82	10010011110
52	11011100010		83	10111100100
53	11011101110		84	10011110100
54	11101011000		85	10011110010
55	11101000110		86	11110100100
56	11100010110		87	11110010100
57	11101101000		88	11110010010
58	11101100010		89	11011011110
59	11100011010		90	11011110110
60	11101111010		91	11110110110
61	11001000010		92	10101111000
62	11110001010		93	10100011110
63	10100110000		94	10001011110
64	10100001100		95	10111101000
65	10010110000		96	10111100010
66	10010000110		97	11110101000
67	10000101100		98	11110100010
68	10000100110		99	10111011110
69	10110010000		CODE B	10111101110
70	10110000100		CODE A	11101011110
71	10011010000		FNC 1	11110101110
72	10011000010		STOP	1100011101011
73	10000110100			Used for Table C
74	10000110010			START 11010011100

TELEPEN™*

TELEPEN takes a much harsher view of the printing technologies than does either UPC or CODE-128. TELEPEN assumes that a coding element will be printed with a width tolerance which might be as bad as ± 50 percent! This assumption stems from an objective of being able to print with elements as small as 0.005 inch (as contrasted to UPC's 0.013″) in order to print the densest possible message. A 50% tolerance makes it impractical to discriminate between bars where one is supposed to be twice the width of some other bar. So the TELEPEN logic is limited to bars or spaces whose widths are either one or three times the widths of the basic element—four different coding components.

As four components require more elements per cipher than do eight components, the TELEPEN system works with 16 elements, whereas CODE-128 achieves the same

*Trademark of SB Electronic Systems, Ltd. Concept of George Simms.

end with only eleven. However, because TELEPEN will stand a width tolerance of 50%, while CODE-128 is limited to 24%, the TELEPEN element can be smaller than the CODE-128 element. In other words, TELEPEN utilizes more smaller elements and gets a higher cipher density thereby.

While TELEPEN ciphers start with a bar and end with a space, as do UPC and CODE-128, the coding combinations range all the way from four wide bars and four narrow spaces (4 × 3 + 4) to eight narrow bars and eight narrow spaces (8 + 8) (see Schedule B.5). This variable bar/space pattern, in contrast to the fixed pattern of both the UPC and CODE-128, leaves the coding more susceptible to spots and voids in the print quality, and deprives the decoding algorithm of one possible safeguard (bar/space pattern check). Further, the cipher for "–" (or 68) is identical to that of START, while the cipher for z (or 95) is identical to that of STOP, which increases the possibility of a substitution error during a skewed or aborted scan.

TELEPEN is a continuous code: the spaces between ciphers are a part of the code.

Schedule B.5.   The TELEPEN cipher set.

START	1010101010111000	S	1010111010111000
STOP	111000101010101	T	1110101110001010
0	1110111010101110	U	1011100010111000
1	1011101000100010	V	1000100010111000
2	1110001000100010	W	1010101110001010
3	1010111010101110	X	1110100010001010
4	1110101000100010	Y	1011101010111000
5	1011100010101110	Z	1110001010101010
6	1000100010101110	a	1011101110101010
7	1010101000100010	b	1110001110101010
8	1110100010100010	c	1010111010001010
9	1011101010101110	d	1110101110101010
A	1011101110111000	e	1011100010001000
B	1110001110111000	f	1000100010001000
C	1010111011101010	g	1010101110101010
D	1110101110111000	h	1110111000101010
E	1011100011101010	i	1011101010001000
F	1000100011101010	j	1110001010001000
G	1010101110111000	k	1010111000101010
H	1110111000111000	l	1110101010001000
I	1011101011101010	m	1010001000101010
J	1110001011101010	n	1000101000101010
K	1010111000111000	o	1010101010001000
L	1110101011101010	p	1110111010101010
M	1010001000111000	q	1011101000101000
N	1000101000111000	r	1110001000101000
O	1010101011101010	s	1010111010101010
P	1110111010111000	t	1110101000101000
Q	1011101110001010	u	1011100010101010
R	1110001110001010	v	1000100010101010

w	1010101000101000	DC2	1110001110001110
x	1110100010101000	DC3	1010111010111010
y	1011101010101010	DC4	1110101110001110
z	1110001010101010	NAK	1011100010111010
!	1011101110101110	SYN	1000100010111010
"	1110001110101110	ETB	1010101110001110
#	1010111011100010	CAN	1110100010001110
$	1110101110101110	EM	1011101010111010
%	1011100011100010	SUB	1110001010111010
&	1000100011100010	ESC	1010100010001110
'	1010101110101110	FS	1110101010111010
(	1110111000101110	GS	1010001010001110
)	1011101011100010	RS	1000101010001110
*	1110001011100010	US	1010101010111010
+	1010111000101110	;	1010100010100010
:	1110000101101110	<	1110101010101110
DEL	1010101010101010	=	1010001010100010
NUL	1110111011101110	>	1000101010100010
SOH	1011101110111010	?	1010101010101110
ETX	1010111011101110	'	1110101011100010
STX	1110001110111010	.	1000101000101110
EOT	1110101110111010	–	1010001000101110
ENQ	1011100011101110	/	1010101011100010
ACK	1000100011101110	\	1110101010111000
BEL	1010101110111010	[	1010100010001010
BS	1110111000111010	]	1010001010001010
HT	1011101011101110	ˆ.	1000101010001010
LF	1110001011101110	—	1010101010111000
VT	1010111000111010	{	1010100010101000
FF	1110101011101110	}	1010001010101000
CR	1010001000111010	|	1110101010101010
SO	1000101000111010	~	1000101010101000
SI	1010101011101110	SP	1110111011100010
DLE	1110111010111010	@	1110111011101010
DC1	1011101110001110	\	1110111010001000

CODE-39™*

CODE-39 (see Fig. B.3) is based on concurrence with the TELEPEN philosophy whereby, as long as printers are idiosyncratic, only four types of coding components are really available: narrow bars, wide bars, narrow spaces, and wide spaces, where the narrow bars (elements) and the narrow spaces (also elements) are the same width, and the wide bars and the wide spaces are also the same width, each of these latter being three times the width of the narrow components (see Fig. B.4).

*Trademark of Interface Mechanisms, Inc. A concept of D. C. Allais.

- • ALPHANUMERIC

- • HIGH SECURITY

- • LOW DENSITY

Figure B.3. CODE-39 characteristics.

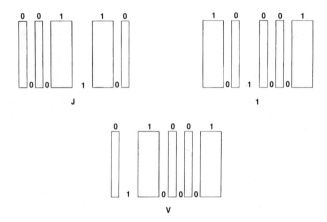

Figure B.4. CODE-39 ciphers.

CODE-39 (see Schedule B.6) consists of:

a 2/5 code   . . . . 2 wides out of 5 bars

combined with

a 1/4 code   . . . . 1 wide out of 4 spaces

to achieve

a 3/9 code   . . . . 3 wides out of 9 components

CODE-39 ciphers start with a bar, end with a bar, and are always printed in the same width—one to every other—in any particular message. Here the spaces between ciphers are unimportant, if separation can be discriminated by the scanning devices, and separation is at least one element wide.

Intermec does not tie down the ratio for wide and narrow components to be used in composing CODE-39 ciphers. They leave it open to lie anywhere between 2.2/1 and 3/1. Because this factor is not tied down, the ability to run elemental parity checks—ones odd and zeros even—is lost.

By assuming a wide/narrow ratio of 3/1, CODE-39 consumes 15 elements in each cipher plus one between ciphers. If this ratio is reduced to 2.2/1 (in order to gain higher packing density), 13 elements are used plus one between each cipher. As a

Schedule B.6.   The Code-39 cipher set.

TWO OF FIVE IMPOSED ON ONE OF FOUR
          CODE*
                          39 ciphers

1	111010001010111	K	111010101000111
2	101110001010111	L	101110101000111
3	111011100010101	M	111011101010001
4	101000111010111	N	101011101000111
5	111010001110101	O	111010111010001
6	101110001110101	P	101110111010001
7	101000101110111	Q	101010111000111
8	111010001011101	R	111010101110001
9	101110001011101	S	101110101110001
0	101000111011101	T	101011101110001
A	111010100010111	U	111000101010111
B	101110100010111	V	100011101010111
C	111011101000101	W	111000111010101
D	101011100010111	X	100010111010111
E	111010111000101	Y	111000101110101
F	101110111000101	Z	100011101110101
G	101010001110111	--	100010101110111
H	111010100011101	.	111000101011101
I	101110100011101	Space	100011101011101
J	101011100011101	*	100010111011101

* Used as START & STOP.

15 elements/cipher plus space

*Intermec calls this code CODE-39 after adding the following "out of pattern" ciphers:

$	100010001000101
/	100010001010001
+	100010100010001
%	101000100010001

Four numbers encoded ((15 + 1) × 6 −1 = 95)
UPC equivalent   ((15 + 1) × 14 −1 = 223)

13-element version cannot achieve the read reliability of a 15-element version, CODE-39 should be considered to consume 16 elements in comparison with other coding systems.

   The fact that the cipher for P is an inversion of the START/STOP cipher is potentially a weak point in the design of CODE-39. This does not cause much of a problem when reading a message printed in high density with a hand-held wand, but it can show up when utilizing low-density printing. This is true because, if the scanning spot of light is able to reverse direction in a space between two ciphers adjacent to a P, it is very possible—depending on the decoding algorithm used—to get a substitution error. This would particularly be true with laser scan, which reverses on a dime at high speed. However, such a substitution can be avoided by using an algorithm which requires extensive white space both before and after each scan. Further, guard lines printed along both top and bottom of a bar-coded message can be used to negate an oblique scan ending or starting with a *P*.

Some of the literature published on CODE-39 claims 43* consistent characters in its cipher set. This is not really true; there are only 39†, because four of those claimed do not conform to the other's coding rules. Codes deviating from a standard pattern impose an unnecessary burden on the decoding algorithms which affects both the first read rate and the substitution error rate.

The dimensional specifications for CODE-39 call for narrow components to be printed with a tolerance of 23% (the same as in the UPC). These close tolerances make possible the specified 2.2/1 wide/narrow ratio. However, if CODE-39 is printed with a 3/1 ratio, much narrower components can be used with a resultant higher cipher density. Certainly the 3/1 ratio should always be used when printing with mechanical dot-matrix printers.

When printing CODE-39 with a serial impact printer, considering mechanical tolerances and anticipated ink spread, the minimum element which can be achieved reliably is probably 0.0075 inch. Assuming a 3/1 ratio, this gives each cipher a nominal width of 0.120 inch. This results in a pitch of 8.3 ciphers per inch. Intermec suggests a 2.24/1 ratio with a density of 9.4 ciphers per inch (see Fig. B.5).

When this code is printed with a mechanical dot-matrix printer of some sort, the cipher density which can be achieved is determined by dot size, the tolerance whereby one dot is laid down in relation to all other dots on a page (registration accuracy), the amount of dot overlap, and the change in dot size with ribbon life. Using a Printronics printer, a nominal bar width of 0.020 inch can be achieved (hammers between 0.017″ and 0.018″, dots overlapping by 50% with a 15% registration accuracy). This results in a cipher density a little more than 3/inch.

CODE-39 is discrete: the spaces between the ciphers are not a part of the code.

- **SERIAL IMPACT — 9.4/"**

- **MECHANICAL MATRIX — 3.5/"**

- **INK-JET — 5-6/"**

- **ELECTROSTATIC — 6-7/"**

- **LASER — 12-16/"**

Figure B.5. CODE-39 density.

*The Material Handling Institute, USD-3.
†The Material Handling Institute, USD-2.

3/9-CODE

Using three wide components (but not limiting these to one wide space and two wide bars), CODE-39 can be expanded to include 80 possible ciphers.

We have said that bar-coding is a method of communicating with computer systems at the local level, as an alternative to keyboards. It might then be asked: why should not bar codes be required to encipher full ASCII? Part of the answer lies in the fact that few computer systems actually involve themselves with full ASCII. Many—indeed most—make out very well with 56 ciphers (½ASCII).

Since, in any system now using CODE-39, CODE-39 can be expanded to THREE-OF-NINE merely through software effort, it seems logical to assume that THREE-OF-NINE is a reasonable response to an ASCII requirement. Certainly, if one can do with 80 ciphers, it offers a much simpler, more read-reliable prospect than either TELEPEN or CODE-128. (See Schedule B.7.)

Schedule B.7. The THREE-OF-NINE CODE cipher set.

CODE-39
As specified by Intermec
(2/5 + 1/4 = 3/9)

M	111011101010001	–	100010101110111
C	111011101000101	7	101000101110111
3	111011100010101	G	101010001110111
W	111000111010101	Q	101010111000111
Y	111000101110101	N	101011101000111
5	111010001110101	D	101011100010111
8	111010001011101	B	101110100010111
.	111000101011101	L	101110101000111
H	111010100011101	2	101110001010111
K	111010101000111	U	111000101010111
1	111010001010111	A	111010100010111
E	111010111000101	4	101000111010111
J	101011100011101	6	101110001110101
J	101110100011101	9	101110001011101
0	101000111011101	F	101110111000101
T	101011101110001	Z	100011101110101
S	101110101110001	Space	100011101011101
R	111010101110001	V	100011101010111
X	100010111010111	O	111010111010001
P	101110111010001	*	100010111011101

Included by Intermec
(0/5 + 3/4 = 3/9)

$	100010001000101	%	101000100010001
/	100010001010001	+	100010100010001

(Continued)

Schedule B.7.   *(Cont.)*

(3/5 + 0/4 = 3/9)

101011101110111	111011101110101
101110101110111	111011101011101
111010101110111	111011101010111

START	101010101000111
STOP	101010101010101

(1/5 + 2/4 = 3/9)

111000100010101	101010001000111
111000101000101	101000101000111
111000101010001	100010101000111
111010001000101	101000100010111
111010100010001	100010001010111
111010001010001	100010100010111
101110001010001	100010100011101
101110100010001	100010001011101
101110001000101	101000100011101
100011101010001	100010101110001
100011101000101	101000101110001
100011100010101	101010001110001
101011100010001	100010001110101
101000111010001	100010111000101
100010111010001	101000111000101

CODE-B

The characteristics of a bar code which determined its read reliability are outlined in Appendix A. From these parameters it should be possible to develop a "basic" code utilizing as many of these features as possible. For instance:

Algorithmic choices of greatest ease:	*Minimum*	*CODE-B*
a. Minimum cipher set	Numeric	10
b. Minimum length of bit-stream	Discrete	9
c. Minimum number of coding components	Two	4
d. Maximum difference between component	Wide/narrow	3/1
e. Shortest pattern of bars or spaces	BSBS	BSBSB

Commonality of Cipher Family:	
a. Standard pattern of bars and spaces	BSBSB
b. Count: Bars	3
Spaces	2
Components	5
Wide components	2

c. Parity: Bars   (components) .... odd
          Spaces (components) .... even
          Zeros (elements) .... even
          Ones   (elements) .... odd

A consideration of all possible code parameters, as listed above, leads to CODE–B, theoretically as well as practically, as the most read-reliable code possible (see Schedule B.8). CODE–B is discrete: the spaces between ciphers are not a part of the code.

Schedule B.8.   The CODE-B cipher set: 10 ciphers.

Character Set	Cipher	Space		Character Set	Cipher	Space
1	111010111	0	unique	6	100010001	0
2	111010001	0	inverse	7	100010111	0
3	111011101	0	inverse	8	101110111	0
4	111000101	0	inverse	9	101000111	0
5	100011101	0	inverse	0	101110001	0
START	101010111	0	unique	STOP	101010101	0

9 elements/cipher + space

Note: CODE-B is a 2/5 code based on a 3/1 width print ratio and uses 59 elements to print ciphers for four numbers ($(9 + 1) \times 6 - 1) = 59$).
UPC equivalent ($(9 + 1) \times 14 - 1 = 139$)

I–2/5–CODE

In the I–2/5–CODE (see Schedule B.9) the bars are coded for those numbers which appear in the odd position of a message, while the spaces (including that space which would otherwise by the space between ciphers) are coded for those numbers which occur in the even positions. This makes possible a superficial comparison to CODE–39 and CODE–B: CODE–39 consumes 16 elements/cipher and CODE–B ten, while I–2/5–CODE gets by with nine (where an element is the narrowest possible bar or space which can be achieved by a particular printing process).

It might thus appear that I–2/5–CODE is the densest possible coding system (as it is now touted in the marketplace). But I–2/5–CODE must always have an even number of ciphers in every message, making the density advantage over CODE–B an illusion in messages which would otherwise use an odd number of ciphers.

An important feature of any bar-code system designed to maximize read reliability is that of a fixed length of bit-stream. Most discrete codes utilize the same number of

Schedule B.9. The I-2/5 CODE cipher set: ten ciphers.

Character Set	Ciphers		Examples
1_1	$111_{000}1_01_01_0111_{000}$	01	10001011101101000
2_2	$1_0111_{000}1_01_0111_{000}$	23	100011100010101110
3_3	$111_{000}111_{000}1_01_01_0$	45	100010111000101110
4_4	$1_01_0111_{000}1_0111_{000}$		
5_5	$111_{000}1_0111_{000}1_01_0$		
6_6	$1_0111_{000}111_{000}1_01_0$		
7_7	$1_01_01_0111_{000}111_{000}$		
8_8	$111_{000}1_01_0111_{000}1_0$		
9_9	$1_0111_{000}1_0111_{000}1_0$		
0_0	$1_01_0111_{000}111_{000}1_0$		

START 1010
STOP 11101

9 elements per cipher

Note: This code is based on a 3/1 width printing ratio and uses 45 elements to print ciphers for four numbers ($4 \times 9 + 4 + 5 = 117$).

bits in each cipher. While the UPC is a continuous code, its fixed message length accomplishes the same end. But fixed-length bit-streams are not a feature of the I-2/5-CODE, so that in systems which must process variable length messages, the I-2/5-CODE has a high cipher-dropout rate.

Another major disadvantage of the I-2/5-CODE is that it costs a great deal more to print than does CODE-B. It cannot be printed by methods which require large, variable-width intercharacter gaps. The sequential numbering wheels on continuous web presses, very large type typewriters, and rubber-belt date stamps and the like, all require a flexible approach to the intercharacter gap.

2/5-CODE*

The basic 2/5-CODE (see Schedule B.10) is similar in structure to CODE-39, except that the spaces are not coded. This is not a very efficient code because, as there must still be spaces between bars at least one element wide, only two elements are saved from the number required by CODE-39. The 2/5-CODE is numeric only.

However, 2/5-CODE is a discrete code where the spaces between ciphers are not important, as long as they are identifiable. The nonsignificance of the space widths is very important in one application. When a laser engraver is used, if the spaces (instead of the bars) are engraved, this code can be laid down much faster than any other code. This can be very important in those circumstances where a bar-code message is incorporated during the manufacturing process.

*A proprietary code of Identicon, Inc. Concept of Gerald Wolff.

Schedule B.10. The 2/5-CODE cipher set: ten ciphers.

Character set	Ciphers
1	1110101010111
2	1011101010111
3	1110111010101
4	1010111010111
5	1110101110101
6	1011101110101
7	1010101110111
8	1110101011101
9	1011101011101
0	1010111011101
START	111011101
STOP	111010111

13 elements per cipher plus space (14 total)

MSI-CODE*

The MSI-CODE (see Schedule B.11) is a continuous, relatively weak code which is inefficient in its use of space. For instance, as a strong, discrete code, CODE-B accomplishes all the same objectives, and much more, in three quarters of the space.

Schedule B.11. The MSI-CODE cipher set: ten ciphers.

	Four of Eight Code 2/1 ratio	*Four of Eight Code* 3/1 ratio
0	100100100100	1000100010001000
1	100100100110	1000100010001110
2	100100110100	1000100011101000
3	100100110110	1000100011101110
4	100110100100	1000111010001000
5	100110100110	1000111010001110
6	100110110100	1000111011101000
7	100110110110	1000111011101110
8	110100100100	1110100010001000
9	110100100110	1110100010001110
	Start = 110	1110
	Stop = 1001	10001

12 (2/1) elements (cipher

Four numbers encoded	$(12 \times 4 + 3 + 4 = 55)$
UPC equivalent	$(12 \times 12 + 3 + 4 = 151)$

*A proprietary code of MSI, Inc.

While this code is unlikely to expand into new applications because of its inherent deficiencies, it has a long history of use (perhaps the longest of all) and, as long as it is perceived to do the job required, is likely to remain an active code.

CODABAR™*

CODABAR (see Schedule B.12) includes a significant element of confusion by mixing two different coding systems with different bit-stream lengths. By this means, it disregards a number of security features which are found in other codes. It is difficult to see how this code can expand into new applications, when other codes are available which can do a much more effective job.

Schedule B.12.   The CODABAR cipher set: 24 ciphers.

Two of Seven Code		*Three of Seven Code*	
0	10101000111	:	1110101110111
1	10101110001	/	1110111010111
2	10100010111	.	1110111011101
3	11100010101	+	1011101110111
4	10111010001	a	1011100010001
5	11101010001	b	1000100010111
6	10001010111	c	1010001000111
7	10001011101	d	1010001110001
8	10001110101	t	1011100010001
9	11101000101	n	1000100010111
–	10100011101	*	1010001000111
$	10111000101	e	1010001110001

CODABAR is a mixture of 2/7 and 3/7 codes.

START/STOP = a/t, b/n, c/* and d/e.

11/13 elements/cipher plus space

Four numbers encoded	((11/13 + 1) × 6 − 1 = 77)
UPC equivalent	((11/13 + 1) × 14 − 1 + 181)

CODE-11†

CODE-11 (see Schedule B.13) is something of a hodgepodge as it draws on five different coding components (1/1, 2/1, and 3/1 bars and 1/1 and 2/1 spaces) which are mixed into two different coding schemes: two-of-five and three-of-five.

*Now under the control of Welch Allyn, Inc.
†A trademark of Interface Mechanisms, Inc. Concept of D. C. Allais.

Schedule B.13.   The CODE-11 cipher set: 11 ciphers.

One of Five Code *3/1 ratio*		*Two of Five Code* *2/1 ration*		

One wide bar   *Two wide bars*

9	1110101	1	1101011
–	1011101	5	1101101
0	1010111	4	1011011

One wide space   *One wide bar, one wide space*

Unused	1000101	2	1001011
Unused	1010001	7	1010011
		8	1101001
		3	1100101
		6	1001101
		START/STOP	10110011

Two spaces
Unused 1001001

7 elements in each cipher plus one element between ciphers

Four numbers encoded	$(7 \times 4 + 7 \times 3 + 6 = 55)$
UPC equivalent	$(7 \times 12 + 7 \times \# + 14 = 105)$

CODE-11 addresses the issue of recording the maximum amount of information in the minimum space. However, because it uses bars of a two-for-one difference in width, it can not be printed with bars as narrow as those which can be used when the difference ratio is three-for-one. As may be seen in the comparison chart of Schedule A.1, both Interleaved Two-of-Five and CODE-B can be printed in higher density.

CODE-11 has been adopted by certain large organizations and, as long as it satisfies them, it will probably not go away. It is a discrete code: the spaces between ciphers are not a part of the code.

TEKSCAN™*

TEKSCAN is a coding technique akin to bar coding (see Schedule B.14 and Fig. B.6). Here the location of an inked mark or "slug," in geographical relation to a reference "backbone" (clock-track equivalent) of other similar slugs, carries the coded information. This technique is aimed at carton identification and in this one application does very well indeed. Individual ciphers are located both on each side of the backbone and extending along the backbone, in some pattern which may be particularly convenient. Various slug combinations are possible in the formulation of a cipher set.

*Trademark of Teknekron, Inc. Concept of Cynthia Ott.

Schedule B.14.   The TEKSCAN cipher set: ten Ciphers.

Character set	Cipher
0	0011
1	0101
2	0110
3	0111
4	1001
5	1010
6	1011
7	1100
8	1101
9	1110

Print stock: white with a *nonreflecting* background opaque enough so that any carton background does not bleed through. Colored stock is also possible, but must be *nonreflective.*
Typical slug size: 0.069 inch wide × 0.095 inch high.
Slug mark color: black.
Typical horizontal spacing of slugs: 0.200 inch, center to center.
Typical vertical spacing of slugs: 0.250 inch, center to center.

Typical reading specifications
    Total depth of field maximum: 30 inches.

    Width of field maximum: 30 inches. (The width of field is defined as an area plus or minus 15 inches from the centerline of the camera.)

    Label rotation: 360°, provided the entire label passes through this field of view and meets the other requirements defined herein.

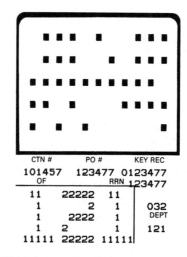

CTN #	PO #	KEY REC
101457	123477	0123477
OF		RRN 123477
11	22222	11	
1	2	1	032
1	2222	1	DEPT
1	2	1	121
11111	22222	11111	

Figure B.6. A TEKSCAN label. Reproduced with permission of Teknekron Controls, Inc.

Consider the TWO-or-THREE-out-of-FOUR version:

- The presence of a slug is a binary one.
- The absence of a slug (where one might otherwise be) is a binary zero.
- Four possible locations are used for each cipher.
- Either TWO or THREE slugs are used to form each cipher.

In any given coded message, a four-bit binary check digit is included. This is alleged to catch up to three "lost" slugs and three "gained" slugs, and to most combinations of errors or false numbers formed by single errors. At the point where the check-digit cannot guarantee catching all errors, the probability of having an illegal two or three out of four code is vanishingly small.

Because TEKSCAN is based on the presence or absence of information, in contrast to a time-increment measurement of bar/space width, it is claimed to have superior read reliability in relation to any other bar-coding technique—a claim that may well be open to argument. Because TEKSCAN utilizes a two-dimensional area, in contrast to other bar-codes' one-dimensional line, it can be read only by some form of area "bit-mapping," which requires quite expensive electronics—Vidicon, Reticon, or swept linear array.

Appendix C
Comparative Statistics

a. Hand-wand reading speed

CODE-39	3–50 inches/second (10–30 most likely)
Magnetic stripe	3–50 inches/second (10–30 most likely)
OCR	3–15 inches/second

b. Beam-scan reading rate

CODE-39	400 hertz
Magnetic-stripe	Not feasible
OCR	Not feasible

c. Automated 6-inch card read rate

CODE-39	100/minute
Magnetic stripe	100/minute
OCR	100/minute

d. Document print rate

Serial impact printer	100 inches/minute
Page printer	50 inches/minute
Ink-jet printer (line)	3,000 inches/minute
Electrostatic stencil	1,200 inches/minute

CODE-39 (2 $\frac{1}{2}$" label)

Serial impact printer	50/minute
Page printer (firmware)	150/minute
Page printer (software)	100/minute
Ink-jet printer	10,000/minute
Electrostatic stencil	4,000/minute

Magnetic stripe

ID card $3/3/8 \times 2\frac{1}{8}$	20/minute
Data card $3\frac{1}{4} \times 5$	18/minute
Data card $3\frac{1}{4} \times 7$	12/minute

OCR ($2\frac{1}{2}''$ label)

Serial impact printer	50/minute
Page printer (firmware)	150/minute
Page printer (software)	100/minute

e. Character set

CODE-39	43 (alphanumeric)
UPC	10 (numeric)
Magnetic stripe (ID card)	30 (partial alphanumeric)
Magnetic stripe (data card)	48 (alphanumeric)
OCR	24 (partial alphanumeric)

f. Cipher density

CODE-39 (serial impact printer)	9.4 ciphers/inch
CODE-39 (page printer)	3.5 ciphers/inch
CODE-39 (ink-jet printer)	5.0 ciphers/inch
Magnetic stripe (ID card)	30/15 ciphers/inch
Magnetic stripe (data card)	10 ciphers/inch
OCR	10 characters/inch

g. Depth of field

Jewel-tip bar-code wand	0.012 inch
Shrouded bar-code wand	0.040 inch (more for special applications)
Magnetic-stripe wand	0.006 inch
OCR wand	0.125 inch
Laser beam	measured in feet

h. Number of passages for manual wand tip (nominal)

Shroud-tip bar-code wand	50,000
Jewel-tip bar-code wand	10,000,000 (claimed)
Magnetic-stripe wand	1,000,000

i. Bidirectional reading

CODE–39	yes
Magnetic-stripe	yes
OCR	yes
Some bar codes	no

j. Data destruction visible

CODE–39	yes
Magnetic stripe	no
OCR	yes

k. Erase and recode

CODE–39	no
Magnetic stripe	yes
OCR	no

l. Cover over coded message

Jewel-tip bar-code wand	0.008 inch
Shroud-tip bar-code wand	0.020 inch
Magnetic-stripe wand	0.002 inch
OCR wand	0.010 inch

m. Long-term deterioration

CODE–39	no
Magnetic stripe	yes
OCR	no

n. Printed on various media

CODE–39	yes
Magnetic stripe	no (by heroic means only)
OCR	yes

o. Copies possible (as contrasted with several originals)

CODE–39	yes
Magnetic stripe	no
OCR	yes

p. Redundancy

CODE-39	multiple scan paths
Magnetic stripe	repeat message
OCR	shape of characters

q. First read rate

CODE-39 on serial impact printer	Above 80%
CODE-39 on page printer	Above 60%
Magnetic stripe	Above 90% (no repeats)
OCR	?

r. Substitution error rate (nominal)

CODE-39 (2 of 5 plus 1 of 4)	1/1,000,000
2/5	1/100,000
UPC	1/50,000
Magnetic stripe	?
OCR	1/10,000

s. Print quality

Serial impact printer	
Carbon ink	Excellent
Noncarbon ink	Good
Vertical matrix printer	
Carbon ink	Not feasible
Noncarbon ink	Poor
Horizontal matrix printer	
Carbon ink	Fair
Noncarbon ink	Fair
Ink-jet printer	
Carbon ink	Excellent
Noncarbon ink	Good
Magnetic stripe	Excellent

t. Print contrast ratio

Carbon inks	
Read with infrared	70–90
Read with visible red	70–85
Read with incandescent	70–85

Carefully chosen noncarbon inks
    Read with visible red   65–85
    Read with incandescent   65–85
Spectrum of noncarbon inks
    Read with visible red   45–65
    Read with incandescent   50–70

u. Maximum character height (available printers)

CODE–39   No limit
Magnetic stripe   0.040 inch
OCR   0.040 inch

v. Skew limitations on wand

CODE–39   None
Magnetic stripe   None
OCR   ± 8°

w. Tilt limitation on wand

CODE–39   as much as 60°
Magnetic stripe   25°
OCR   15°

x. Contamination of message

Infrared bar-code wand   Reads through matter not absorbing IR.
Visible red bar-code wand Reads through matter not absorbing VR.
Incandescent bar-code wand Duplicates what is seen by human eye, more or less.
Magnetic stripe   Erased by magnetic field of less than 300 gauss. Obscured by magnetic dust.
OCR   Reads through matter not absorbing IR.

y. Spectral regions

Visible range   400–700 nanometers
Deep red   700 NM
Red   656 NM
Yellow   589 NM
Blue   486 NM
Violet   396 NM

Appendix D
Vendors

Hand-Held Wand Scanners

AMES COLOR FILE
12 Park Street
Somerville, MA 02143
(617) 776-1142

AZUR-DATA
4102 148th Avenue, NE
Redmond, WA 98052
(206) 881-5100

COMPUTER IDENTICS CORPORATION
5 Shawmut Road
Canton, MA 02021
(617) 821-0830

COMPUTER SYSTEMS ENGINEERING
16 Second Avenue
Burlington, MA 01803
(617) 272-4348

CONTROL MODULE
380 Enfield Street
Enfield, CT 06082
(203) 745-2433

DATALOGIC OPTIC ELECTRONICS, INC.
2904 Southwood Drive
Westlake, OH 44145
(216) 871-0604

HEWLETT-PACKARD OPTOELECTRONICS
640 Page Mill Road
Palo Alto, CA 94304
(415) 857-1501

CASIO, INC.
15 Gardner Road
Fairfield, NJ 07006
(201) 575-7400 (U.S. sales office)

INTERTELEPHON
1185 Terra Bella Avenue
Mountain View, CA 94043
(415) 961-3952

INTERFACE MECHANISMS, INC.
4405 Russell Road
Lynnwood, WA 98036
(206) 743-7036

SB ELECTRONIC SYSTEMS, LTD.
Davenport House
Bowers Way
Harpenden
Hertfordshire AL54HY
England
Harpenden 05827-69991

SKAN-A-MATIC CORPORATION
P.O. Box S
Elbridge, NY 13060
(315) 689-3961

WELCH ALLYN
Industrial Products Division
Jordan Road
Skaneateles Falls, NY 13153
(315) 685-8351

MICRONICS, AB
Box 2071
S-18302 TABY
Stockholm, Sweden
(312) 451-9191 (U.S. sales office)

PLESSEY COMMUNICATIONS SYSTEMS, LTD.
Beeston, Nottingham N69 1LA
England
(0602) 254822

Fixed-beam/Slot Scanners

MEKONTROL, INC.
56 Hudson Street
Northboro, MA 01532
(617) 393-2451

COMPUTER SYSTEMS ENGINEERING
16 Second Avenue
Burlington, MA 01803
(617) 272-4348

ELECTRONICS CORPORATION OF AMERICA
Photoswitch Division
1 Memorial Drive
Cambridge, MA 02142
(617) 864-8000

SICK OPTIK-ELECTRONIK, INC.
2059 White Bear Avenue
St. Paul, MN 55109
(612) 777-9453

SCOPE, INC.
1860 Michael Faraday Drive
Reston, VA 22090
(703) 471-5600

ACCU-SORT SYSTEMS
511 School House Road
Telford, PA 18969
(215) 723-0981

Laser Scanners

ACCU-SORT SYSTEMS
511 School House Road
Telford, PA 18969
(215) 723-0981

COMPUTER IDENTICS CORPORATION
5 Shawmut Road
Canton, MA 02021
(617) 821-0830

CONTROL MODULE
380 Enfield Street
Enfield, CT 06082
(203) 745-2433

DATALOGIC OPTIC ELECTRONICS, INC.
2904 Southwood Drive
Westlake, OH 44145
(216) 871-0604

MRC CORPORATION
Scanner Systems Division
11212 McCormick Road
Hunt Valley, MD 21031
(301) 628-1300

METROLOGIC INSTRUMENTS, INC.
143 Harding Avenue
Bellmawr, NJ 08031
(609) 933-0100

MICROSCAN SYSTEM, INC.
432 Lakeside Drive
Sunnyvale, CA 94086
(408) 733-4200

SCOPE, INC.
1860 Michael Faraday Drive
Reston, VA 22090
(703) 471-5600

SKAN-A-MATIC CORPORATION
P.O. Box S
Elbridge, NY 13060
(315) 689-3961

SYMBOL TECHNOLOGIES, INC.
90 Plant Avenue
Hauppauge, NY 11787
(516) 231-5252

SPECTRA PHYSICS, INC.
959 Terry Street
Eugene, OR 97402
(800) 547-2507

CONTROL LASER, INC.
11222 Astronaut Boulevard
Orlando, FL 32809
(305) 851-2540

COGNEX, INC.
1505 Commonwealth Avenue
Boston, MA 02135
(617) 254-1231

REXNORD, INC.
P.O. Box 2022
4701 W. Greenfield Avenue
Milwaukee, WI 53201

Point-of-Sale Scanners

SPECTRAPHYSICS, INC.
333 N. First Street
San Jose, CA 95134
(408) 946-6080

NCR
Cambridge, OH
(614) 439-0594

IBM
Data Processing Division
1133 Westchester Avenue
White Plains, NY 10604

SPERRY-UNIVAC
P.O. Box 500
Blue Bell, PA
(215) 542-4011

REXNORD
Recognition Systems Division
4701 N. Greenfield Avenue
Milwaukee, WI 53214
(414) 643-3252

MICROSCAN SYSTEM, INC.
6810 Roswell Road
NW Suite 2a
Atlanta, GA 30328
(404) 393-3060

SWEDA
4000 Dusseldorf-Heerdt
Am Heerdter Hof 11-13
Postfach 5128
02 11/50 82-1
West Germany

Hand-Held Scanner

METROLOGIC INSTRUMENTS, INC.
Scanner Division
143 Harding Avenue
Bellmawr, NJ 08031
(609) 933-0100

SYMBOL TECHNOLOGIES, INC.
90 Plant Avenue
Hauppauge, NY 11787
(516) 231-5252

CONTROL LASER CORPORATION
11222 Astronaut Boulevard
Orlando, FL 32809
(305) 851-2540

NORAND, INC.
550 Second Street, NE
Cedar Rapids, IA 52401
(319) 366-7611

DATALOGIC OPTIC ELECTRONIC, INC.
20340 Center Ridge Road
Rocky River, OH 44116

OCR Hand-Held Wands

CAERE CORPORATION
100 Cooper Court
Los Gatos, CA 95030
(408) 395-7000

RECOGNITION EQUIPMENT, INC.
P.O. Box 222307
Dallas, TX 75222
(214) 579-6000

DATA COPY CORPORATION
1070 East Meadow Circle
Palo Alto, CA 94303
(415) 493-3420

SIEMENS AKTIENGESELLSCHAFT
Postfach 7000072
D-8000
Munchen 70 West Germany

KEYTRONIC, INC.
P.O. Box 14687
Spokane, WA 99214
(509) 928-8000

OCR Page Readers

COGNITRONICS, INC.
25 Crescent Street
Stamford, CT 06906
(203) 327-5307

DEST DATA CORPORATION
1285 Forgewood Avenue
Sunnyvale, CA 94086
(408) 734-1234

KEY TRONIC, INC.
P.O. Box 14687
Spokane, WA 99214
(509) 928-8000

CONTEXT CORPORATION
(A division of Burroughs)
9 Ray Avenue
Burlington, MA 01803
(617) 273-2222

AMER-O-MATIC CORPORATION
P.O. Box 2247
Birmingham, AL 35201
(205) 252-5177

Mechanical Dot-Matrix Line Printers

PRINTRONIX, INC.
17421 Derian Avenue
Irvine, CA 92714
(714) 549-8272

OKIDATA CORPORATION
111 Gaither Drive
Mt. Laurel, NY 08054
(609) 235-2600

TALLY
(A division of Mannesmann)
8301 South 180th Street
Kent, WA 98031
(206) 251-5500

NCR CORPORATION
950 Danby Road
Ithaca, NY 14850
(607) 273-5310

Mechanical Dot-Matrix Character Printers

CENTRONICS DATA COMPUTER CORPORATION
Route III
Hudson, NH 03051
(603) 883-0111

DATAPRODUCTS
6219 DeSoto Avenue
Woodland Hills, CA 91365
(213) 887-8000

LEAR SIEGLER, INC.
Data Products Division
714 North Brookhurst Street
Anaheim, CA 92803
(714) 774-1010

FLORIDA DATA CORPORATION
3308 New Haven Avenue
West Melbourne, FL 32901
(305) 724-6088

SANDERS TECHNOLOGY
Columbia Drive
Amherst, NH 03061
(603) 882-1000

GENERAL ELECTRIC
Data Communication Products
Business Department
Waynesboro, VA 22980
(703) 942-8161

MANNESMANN TALLY
8301 South 180th Street
Kent, WA 98031
(206) 251-5500

PANNIER, INC.
207 Sandusky St.
Pittsburgh, PA 15212
(412) 323-4900

DATA SPECIALISTS, INC.
3455 Commercial Ave.
Northbrook, IL 60062
(312) 564-1800

Ink-Jet Line Printers

A. B. DICK COMPANY
Information Products Division
220 Arthur Avenue
Elk Grove Village, IL 60007
(312) 593-8800

MEAD CORPORATION
3800 Space Drive
P.O. Box 3230
Dayton, OH 45431
(513) 898-3644

MARSH STENCIL MACHINE COMPANY
Belleville, IL 62222
(618) 234-1122

Ink-Jet Character Printers

SIEMENS AKTIENGESELLSCHAFT
Postfach 7000072
D-8000
Munchen 70 West Germany

PRINTA COLOR, INC.
P.O. Box 52
Norcross, GA 30091
(404) 448-2675

Electrostatic Line Printers

MARKEM CORPORATION
150 Congress Street
Keene, NH 03431
(603) 352-1130

MAGNESTYLUS PRODUCTS DIVISION
3M Co.
Building 220
8 East
3M Center
St. Paul, MN 55101
(800) 328-1300

XEROX CORPORATION
Versatec Division
2805 Bowers Avenue
Santa Clara, CA 95051
(408) 988-2800

DENNISON MANUFACTURING COMPANY
300 Howard Street
Framingham, MA 01701
(617) 879-0511

Laser Printers

CANON USA, INC.
LBP Department
1 Canon Plaza
Lake Success, NY 11042
(516) 488-6700

HEWLETT-PACKARD
640 Page Mill Road
Palo Alto, CA 94304
(415) 857-1501

IBM
Old Orchard Road
Armonk, NY 10504
(914) 765-1900

Serial Impact Printers

INTERFACE MECHANISMS, INC.
4405 Russell Road
Lynnwood, WA 98036
(206) 743-7036

ESSELTE METO INTERNATIONAL Gmbh
Postfach 1100
D-6932
Hirshhorn/N Brentano Strasse
West Germany
06272/631

Thermal Printers

INTERFACE MECHANISMS, INC.
4405 Russell Road
Lynnwood, WA 98036
(206) 743-7036

BIZERBA, Werke Wilhelm Kraut Gmbh
Waagen und Maschinen Fabriken
Postfach 1140
7460 Balingen
West Germany
07433/121

MATTHEWS INTERNATIONAL, INC.
1910 Cochran Road
Manor Oak 11, Suite 638
Pittsburgh, PA 15220
(412) 344-9433

Laser Engravers

KORAD LASER SYSTEMS
2520 Colorado Avenue
Santa Monica, CA 90404
(213) 829-3377

LUMONICS RESEARCH, LTD.
Lasermark Division
105 Schneider Road
Kanata (Ottawa)
Ontario, Canada K2K 1Y3
(613) 592-1460

CONTROL LASER, INC.
Holobeam Laser, Inc.
P.O. Box 13390
Orlando, FL 32809
(305) 851-2540

QUANTRAD CORPORATION
19900 S. Normandie Avenue
Torrance, CA 90502
(213) 538-9800

GENERAL PHOTONICS
2255 F Martin Avenue
Santa Clara, CA 95050
(408) 496-6040

MARKEM CORPORATION
Keene, NH 03431
(603) 352-1130

LASER IDENTIFICATION SYSTEMS, INC.
9252 Deering Avenue
Chatsworth, CA 91311
(213) 709-1222

Carton Printing

INDUSTRIAL MARKING EQUIPMENT COMPANY,
INC.
4385 Westroads Drive
West Palm Beach, FL 33407
(305) 845-2828

PACKAGING SERVICE INDUSTRIES
315-27th Avenue, N.E.
Minneapolis, MN 55418
(612) 340-6222

PACKAGE PRODUCTS COMPANY
(A division of Engraph, Inc.)
P.O. Box 32816
Charlotte, NC 28232
(704) 377-2691

MATTHEWS INTERNATIONAL CORPORATION
6515 Penn Avenue
Pittsburgh, PA 15206
(412) 665-2500

MARSH STENCIL MACHINE COMPANY
707 East B Street
P.O. Box 388
Belleville, IL 62222
(618) 234-1122

SYMBOLOGY, INC.
P.O. Box 8162
St. Paul, MN 55113
(612) 631-0520

Label Certification Instruments

RJS ENTERPRISES, INC.
135 E. Chestnut Avenue
Monrovia, CA 91016
(213) 357-9781

METROLOGIC INSTRUMENTS, INC.
143 Harding Avenue
Bellmawr, NJ 08031
(609) 933-0100

PHOTOGRAPHIC SCIENCES CORPORATION
770 Basket Road
P.O. Box 338
Webster, NY 14580
(716) 265-1600

SKAN-A-MATIC CORPORATION
P.O. Box S
Elbridge, NY 13060
(315) 689-6751

ERGI Gmbh
Otto-Rohm Strasse 81
D-6100 Darmstadt
West Germany
(06151) 86269

GENERAL GRAPHICS, INC.
327 East Sixth Avenue
Tarentum, PA 15084

SYMBOL TECHNOLOGIES, INC.
90 Plant Avenue
Hauppauge, NY 11787
(516) 231-5252

Labels/Label Stock

H. W. BRADY COMPANY
727 W. Glendale Avenue
P.O. Box 571
Milwaukee, WI 53201
(414) 332-8100

DENNISON MANUFACTURING COMPANY
Identification Systems Division
Framingham, MA 01701
(617) 879-0511

AVERY INTERNATIONAL
415 Huntington Drive
San Marino, CA 91108
(213) 799-0881

COMPUTYPE, INC.
2285 West County Road C
St. Paul, MN 55113
(612) 633-0633

WEBER MARKING SYSTEMS
711 W. Algonquin Road
Arlington Heights, IL 60005
(312) 364-8500

ENGRAPH, INC.
P.O. Box 32816
Charlotte, NC 28232
(704) 377-3621

3M COMPANY
Industrial Tape Division
Building 220-8E
3M Center
St. Paul, MN 55101
(612) 733-6404

GRAND RAPIDS LABEL
2351 Oak Industrial Drive
Grand Rapids, MI 49505
(616) 459-8134

LORD LABEL SYSTEMS, INC.
1200 Avenue H East
Arlington, TX 76011
(214) 647-2504

MARKEM CORPORATION
150 Congress Street
Keene, NH 03431
(603) 352-1130

YORK TAPE AND LABEL CORPORATION
P.O. Box 1309
York, PA 17405
(714) 846-4840

Label Application Systems

LORD LABEL SYSTEMS, INC.
1200 Avenue H. East
Arlington, TX 76011
(214) 647-2504

MARKEM, INC.
150 Congress Street
Keene, NH 03431
(603) 352-1130

Miscellaneous

THE STANDARD REGISTER COMPANY
P. O. Box 1167
Dayton OH 45401
(513) 223-6186
(Label preparation systems)

QED SYSTEMS, INC.
1616 Maplewood Drive, N.E.
Cedar Rapids, IA 52402
(319) 364-4384
(Consultants)

DYMARC INDUSTRIES, INC.
7133 Rutherford Road
Baltimore, MD 21207
(301) 298-3130
(Software)

RECALL SYSTEMS, INC.
306 Kennedy Road
Los Gatos, CA 95030
(408) 356-5462
(Consultants)

TECHNICAL ANALYSIS CORPORATION
W. 120 W. Wieuca Road N.E.
Manor Oak Two Suite 638
Atlanta, GA 30042
(404) 252-1045
(Consultants)

TEKNEKRON CONTROLS INCORPORATED
2121 Allston Way
Berkeley, CA 94704
(415) 843-8227
(Systems)

FAIRCHILD, INC.
464 Ellis St.
Mountain View, CA 94042
(415) 962-5011
(Linear arrays)

MICRONICS AB
Box 2071, S-18302 TABY
Stockholm, Sweden
(312) 451-9191
(Data entry)

NORTH AMERICAN TECHNOLOGY
174 Concord Street
The Strand Building
Peterborough, NH 03458
(603) 924-6048
(Consultants/software)

GEORGE LITHO CORPORATION
650 Second Street
San Francisco, CA 94107
(415) 397-2400
(Typesetters)

MATTHEWS INTERNATIONAL CORPORATION
1910 Cochran Road
Pittsburgh, PA 15220
(800) 245-1168
(Print plates/film masters)

WAKEFIELD SOFTWARE SYSTEMS
28 D Vernon Street
Wakefield, MA 01880
(617) 246-2200
(Software)

COMMUNICATIONS STRATEGY, LTD.
25 Bedford Square
London, WC1, England
01/637-8481
(Systems)

DATA COMPOSITION, INC.
1099 Essex
Richmond, CA 94801
(415) 232-6200
(Plates, labels, ID cards)

LORD LABEL SYSTEMS, INC.
1200 Avenue H East
Arlington, TX 76011
(214) 647-2504
(Labeling systems)

HI-SPEED CHECKWEIGHER COMPANY, INC.
605 West State Street
P.O. Box 40
Ithaca, NY 14850
(607) 273-5704
    (Labeling equipment)

LEUE MANAGEMENT CONSULTANTS
6419 Haunetal
Ilmesmuhle, West Germany
(06673) 1221
    (Consultants)

CREATIVE DATA SERVICES, INC.
100 Progress Parkway, Suite 111
Maryland Heights, MO 63043
    (Consultants)

NEW BRUNSWICK INTERNATIONAL, INC.
5 Greek Lane
Edison, NJ 08817
(201) 287-2288
    (Printer)

COMPUTYPE, INC.
2285 West County Road C
St. Paul, MN 55113
(612) 633-0633
    (Labels)

COMPUTER DEVICES, INC.
25 North Avenue
Burlington, MA 01803
(617) 273-1550
    (Systems)

PRODUCT IDENTIFICATION, INC.
525 N. Fox Hills Dr.
Bloomfield Hills, MI 48013
(313) 334-8838
    (Systems)

KPG
6075 Barfield Road, N.E.
Atlanta, GA 30328
(404) 252-7366
    (Systems)

WESTERN COMPUTER SYSTEMS, INC.
P.O. Box 10191
Eugene, OR 97440
(503) 485-5222
    (Systems)

SATO (OF JAPAN)
One First Street
Los Altos, CA 94022
(415) 948-3911
    (Printers)

Appendix E
Bibliography

Publications

CONTEMPORARY APPLICATIONS OF OPTICAL
BAR CODE TECHNOLOGY
Banks, Helmers & Trueblood
North American Technology, Inc.
Strand Building
174 Concord Street
Peterborough, NH 03458
(603) 924-7136

BAR CODE SCANNING—REFERENCE GUIDE
MSI Data Corporation
340 Fischer Avenue
Costa Mesa, CA 92626
(714) 549-6000

OPTOELECTRONICS DESIGNER'S CATALOG
Hewlett-Packard Company
640 Page Mill Road
Palo Alto, CA 94304
(415) 857-1501

HEWLETT-PACKARD JOURNAL
January 1981

OCR WAND READER MEDIA MANUAL
Recognition Equipment, Inc.
P.O. Box 222307
Dallas, TX 75222
(214) 579-6000

OPTOELECTRONIC DESIGN CONSIDERATIONS
FOR A BAR CODE DATA ENTRY SYSTEM
R. L. Krause
Hewlett-Packard
1850 Embarcadero Road
Palo Alto, CA 94303
(415) 857-6392

ALL ABOUT OPTICAL READERS

UNIVERSAL VENDOR MARKETING FOR THE
GENERAL MERCHANDISE INDUSTRY

A BUYER'S BUIDE TO INTEGRATED POS SYSTEMS

APPLICATION FOR INTEGRATED POS SYSTEMS
FOR THE GENERAL MERCHANDISE INDUSTRY
Datapro Report
1805 Underwood Boulevard
Delran, NY 08075

ELECTRONIC PRINTER INDUSTRY SERVICE
Dataquest Report
19055 Pruneridge Avenue
Cupertino, CA 95014
(408) 725-1200

BAR CODES—AUTOMATIC PRODUCTION COST
CUTTERS
Production Engineering
April 1982
R. C. Rodgers

BAR CODE SYSTEMS—MARKET FORECAST
Craig Harmon
QED Systems, Inc.
1616 Maplewood Drive, N.E.
Cedar Rapids, IA 52402
(319) 364-4384

PRODUCTION & INVENTORY MANAGEMENT
REVIEW
June 1982

ELEMENTS OF A BAR CODE SYSTEM
Hewlett-Packard
Application Notes 1013

Standardizing Organizations

RECOGNITION TECHNOLOGIES USERS
ASSOCIATION
Box 2016
Manchester Center, VT 05255
(802) 262-4151

COUNCIL FOR PERIODICAL DISTRIBUTER
ASSOCIATIONS
488 Madison Avenue
New York, NY 10002
(212) 371-7442

INSTITUTE OF PACKAGING
Fountain House
1a Elm Park
Stanmore, Middlesex
HA7 4BZ England

NATIONAL RETAIL MANUFACTURER'S
ASSOCIATION
100 West 31st Street
New York, NY 10001
(212) 244-8780

AMERICAN NATIONAL STANDARDS INSTITUTE
1430 Broadway
New York, NY 10018
(212) 354-3300

AMERICAN BLOOD COMMISSION
1901 North Fort Myer Drive
Suite 300
Arlington, VA 22209
(703) 522-8414

UPC—UPC SYMBOL SPECIFICATION
Uniform Product Code Council, Inc.
7061 Corporate Way
Suite 106
Dayton, OH 45479
(513) 435-3870

USD-1 (I-2/5 CODE)

USD-2 (CODE-39 RESTRICTED)

USD-3 (CODE-39)

USD-4 (CODABAR)
The Material Handling Institute
1326 Freeport Road
Pittsburgh, PA 15238
(412) 782-1624

UNIFORM CONTAINER SYMBOL
Fibre Box Association
5725 East River Road
Chicago, IL 60631
(312) 693-9600

LOGMARS REPORT
Director, DARCOM Packaging, Storage
and Containerization Center
Tobyhana Army Depot
Tobyhana, PA 18466
(717) 894-7144
    Attention: SDS-TO-TP

AUTOMOTIVE INDUSTRY ACTION GROUP
Project Team on Bar Coding
466 Stephenson Highway
Troy, MI 48084
    Chairmen: Jack Loeffler (313) 322-1360
              Don Dubuc   (313) 575-1493

AUSTRALIAN MEAT PACKERS STANDARDS
CSIRO
Meat Research Laboratory
P.O. Box 12,
Cannon Hill
Australia 4170
(07) 399-3122

Code Control Organizations

BAR CODE	REFERENCE
MSI-Code	MSI Data Corporation
	340 Fischer Avenue
	Costa Mesa, CA 92626
	(714) 549-6000
CODABAR	Welch Allyn, Inc.
	Skaneateles Falls
	NY 13153
	(314) 685-8351
UPC	UPC Counsel, Inc.
	7061 Corporate Way
	Dayton, OH 45459
	(513) 435-3870
CODE-39	Interface Mechanisms,
CODE-11	Inc.
CODE-13	P.O. Box N
CODE-93	Lynnwood, WA 98036
	(206) 743-7036
2/5-CODE	Identicon, Inc.
	1 Kenwood Circle
	Franklin, MA 02038
	(617) 528-6500
CODE-128	Computer Identics,
	Inc.
	31 Dartmouth Street
	Westwood, MA 02090
	(617) 329-1980
TELEPEN	SB Electronic Systems
	Limited
	Davenport House
	Bowers Way
	Harpendend
	Herfordshire AL54HY
	England
	Harpenden (05827)
	69991

EAN	EAN Association
	Rue des Colonies 1000
	28 Bte—8
	Brussels, Belgium
TEKSCAN	Teknekron Controls,
	Inc.
	2121 Allston Way
	Berkeley, CA 94704
	(415) 843-8227
MIL-STD-129H	U.S. Department of
	Defense
MIL-STD-1189	Director, DARCOM
	Tobyhana Army Depot
	Tobyhana, PA 18466
	(714) 894-7144

Newsletters

SCAN, a division of GGX Associates, Inc.
11 Middle Neck Road
Great Neck, NY 11021
(516) 487-6370

AIAG NEWSLETTER
C/O Nitkorski, Douglas & Lomason
24600 Hallwood Court
Farmington Hills, MI 48018

RETAIL AUTOMATION
RMDP, 5/6 East Street
Brighton, Sussex
BNI 1HP England

BAR CODE NEWS
174 Concord Street
Peterborough, NH 03458
(603) 924-6048

Appendix F
Production Control

Production control might be defined as the art of merging hierarchies of authority, skill, process, configuration, function, time, and space into one interrelated system of productivity. The complexity of this art is reflected in the construction of the data base used in its support.

Breaking the overall production problem down into manageable portions—work orders, work units, work pieces, work intervals, work stations—is an originating task of production control. Once these portions are defined and quantified, *transaction descriptions* are used to tune a system to some rhythm of maximized productivity. These preestablished transaction descriptions are a means of both scheduling work units (WHEN/times), and of routing work pieces (WHERE/locations).

However, control does not necessarily follow either definition or direction intent. Control is a process of making things happen. In this context, control follows an ability to relate actual transactions to those intended. This is possible only where descriptions of actual transactions are collected, and where these descriptions are compared to the descriptions of projected transactions within a time interval compatible with causative action. Considering the quantity of data involved, and the time available for effective action, today's production control must be computer-derived. That is, both a full description of production control's intentions, and a description of actual performance, must be lodged in computer memory organized as a data base.

TRANSACTIONS

Production control objectives involve the manipulation of two basic elements: work pieces and work units. A work unit is used to either move or transform a work piece. The work unit concept implies the passage of time—a work interval. A work unit is therefore defined by two transactions, one initiating a work interval and the other defining its end. The detailed description of each such transaction is completed by the traditional WHEN/time, WHERE/location, WHAT/work piece, and WHO/worker. The HOW is of course a description of the work unit itself. Sometimes only God knows WHY!)

In the manufacturing milieu, transaction descriptions perform two basic functions:

First, descriptions of actual transactions collected in real time provide a picture of progress—a snapshot of the real world. Second, projected transaction descriptions communicate Production Control's intentions to those individuals who are expected to perform work.

If work performance is to be maximized, it must be possible to project intentions from a computer-lodged data base into the areas where work is actually performed. This is accomplished either by on-line tutorial terminals located in the work areas, or by preprinted documents which somehow are made to arrive in appropriate work areas prior to scheduled performance. Each individual worker therefore receives instructions either by document or from terminal display.

HISTORY

In the bad old pioneering days, computer operators' primary concerns centered on the horrors of machine language and on the problems of replacing failed vacuum tubes fast enough to achieve useful up-times. By the mid-1960s, the up-time problem was pretty well resolved with components stemming from the semiconductor revolution, whereby large, central key-punch operations with highly trained staffs translated documents of all kinds (gathered from many sources) into the hollerith, punched-card formats which computers could then accept in lieu of machine language.

Today the hollerith card is fast going the way of vacuum tubes. In a production control climate, extensive use is now made of key-memory systems wherein information is introduced directly into computer memory (often disk memory) from manually operated keyboards. This has been called "distributed data processing" because information of interest is derived from many widely distributed terminals. However, "distributed" in the above sense is only relative, as these terminals are commonly located in work centers each of which serves several work stations. A worker must then leave his work station and go to a work center in order to communicate with a computer. A present objective is to locate terminals directly in work stations and to collect as much information as possible about work-station activities by automated, in contrast to manual, means.

DATA BASE

In traditional thought, an electronically maintained *data base* is viewed as a library. An interested individual approaches such a library via a terminal to either add or retrieve data, much as one might check out or return a book in a conventional library. In an electronic library the supported information moves back and forth between appropriate terminals and the centralized retentive media—core, disk, and tape—and is further shuttled around among these various media by internally responsive program instructions.

In contrast, in a factory environment with many terminals distributed out on the factory floor, it is useful to consider a data base as if it too were spread out over the factory floor. Here the retained information extends well beyond any centrally located memory form. Information is represented by work pieces, documents, and the like, and the information flows from these media to the magnetic media and back as directed by various programmed transactions. The structure of these transactions, both from a physical and a logical standpoint, determines the effectiveness of this concept. Such effectiveness is maximized when the logical structure of the transactions is consistent with the logical construction of the data base in toto. (See Schedule F.1.)

Schedule F.1.   Data-base construction.

CONTROL	(Production control)	
REFERENCE	Address to data base	
Revision	To schedule	
Split		
AUTHORITY	(Department/work-center control)	
Purchase order/s	Source/s funds	
Job order/s	MIS Plex file address	
WORK ORDER	Plex authority to perform work – – – – – – – – – – – – –	
Category	Attribute/key—type funding, priority	
Revision	To subschedule	
CONFIGURATION	(WHAT—Tree/Plex)	
Raw stock	Root	
Subassembly	Tree-down	
ENTITY		
PART NUMBER	Entity identifier – – – – – – – – – – – – – – – – –	
Category	Attribute/key—color, code, etc.	
Drawing	Number/header	
Alternative	As built, substitute, etc.	
Next assembly	Plex/Tree-up	
Product/s	Plex/Tree-top	
QUANTITY		
Required	By job order	
COMPLETED	Actual number – – – – – – – – – – – – – – – – – –	
Verified	Inspected, tested, etc.	
Scrapped		
Short		
Split		
TRAJECTORY	(WHERE—Route)	
Source		
Previous location		Example of a
CURRENT LOCA-		COMPLETE
TION		Transaction
Plant		
Department		
Work center		
WORK STATION –		
Bin/s, Shelf/s, etc.		
Destination		
Ultimate destination		
Split		
STAFF	(WHO—Security)	
WORKER	Identification—card, pass-word, etc. – – – – – – – – – – –	
Category	Attribute/key—type required	
TIMING	(WHEN—Schedule)	
Issued		
Required		
Work unit started		
Work unit interrupted		
Work unit restarted		
WORK UNIT COM-		
PLETED –		
Split		
OPERATIONS	(HOW—Consequences)	
Actual work interval		
Standard work interval		
Actual cost		
Standard cost		
Process category	Attribute/key—type	
Instructions	Header	

Appendix G
Glossary

Here are offered not only definitions for many terms used in the text, but concepts which relate the data base of a computer system to that portion of such a data base represented by all the items—documents, materials, parts, locations, and the like—distributed over a factory floor.

Aberration. A departure from intention.

Aberration Report. A report of actual performance when such performance differs from the intended performance.

Access Alternative. A process whereby, when access to current memory is blocked, nonvalidated transaction descriptions are logged and later recovered for reconstruction purposes.

Access Method. A technique for seeking, reading, or writing data on a storage unit.

Account Period. An increment of time during which events of interest take place. Here the catalog of such events is referenced to the account period rather than to the actual times of occurrence.

Account Period Polling. The arrangement, in a computer-directed system, whereby each data-collection point is queried (polled) at the end of an account period. This is in contrast to a system which polls every data-collection point at a rate fast enough to collect any event description at the time of actual occurrence at any collection point.

Actuator. Mechanism for moving or controlling something indirectly instead of by hand.

Address. Key used to assign locations for record storage.

Algorithm. A mathematical process whereby a conclusion is reached as a result of following a progressive series of logical, preestablished propositions each one of which, in regularized sequence, calls for a decision—a choice between various possibilities.

A step-by-step procedure for solving a problem or accomplishing some end.

Alphanumeric Bar Code. A mixture of bar configurations representing alphabetic and numeric symbols.

ASCII. The code described in *American National Standard Code Information Interchange,* ANSI X3.4–1968, used for information interchange among data-processing systems, communication systems, and associated equipment. The ASCII set consists of control characters and graphic characters.

A/S–R/S. *Automatic Storage/Retrieval Systems.*

Aspect Ratio. The ratio of height to width of a bar-code symbol. A code twice as high as wide would have an aspect ratio of 2; a code twice as wide as high would have an aspect ratio of 0.5.

Assigned Bit. Either a bar or a space which is assigned zero or one significance because of its particular width.

Attribute. A quality describing an entity. A "column" relationship in a multicolumn tabulation.

Audit. Querying of a data base, for which physical memory divided into noncontiguous segments is required. One segment holds a description of the data base as it was at the start of the audit period; a second maintains the current description; a third represents a log of changes as these occur during the audit period; while a fourth logs complete transaction descriptions.

An audit can be performed only for those periods where transaction logs are maintained.

Audit Period. Same as "account period."

Automatic Action. Mechanical action having a self-acting or self-regulating mechanism.

Automatic Read. The reading of a bar-code message by some automated means, either beam-scanning or linear array.

Automation. The technique of making an apparatus, a process, or a system operate automatically.

Background Reflectance. Measurement of the brightness or reflectance of the substrate that a bar code is printed on.

Bad Read. Data output condition where the scanned data does not agree with the printed message.

Bar. One single horizontal or vertical line.

Bar Code. Ciphers constructed from a series of dark and light bars organized, according to specific rules, into various patterns which represent letters, numerals, and other human-readable symbols. Coding variables include the number of dark bars, the relative positions of dark bars within a code structure, the variable widths of the dark bars, the variable widths of the light bars, and their relative positions.

Bar-Code Density. The number of characters that a code can represent, per linear inch.

Bar-Code Header Printer. A device to print bar-code headers along one edge of a document of any size.

Bar-Code Symbol. The entire symbol, made up of several bar-code ciphers, which stands for a complete product number, etc.

Bar Coding. A means for the deferred transfer of information from one computer to another via a printed image without detailed processing or transcribing by a human operator.

Bar Length. Measurement of the long dimension of a bar.

Bar Ratio. A particular bar code's relationship of the stroke width of the narrow bars (white or black) to the wide bars.

Bar Width. Measurement of the thickness or width of a bar.

Bar Width Reduction. Deliberate reduction of the width of bars on film masters or printing plates, to compensate for the gain in bar width that takes place during printing. Correct use of bar width reduction results in printed bar-code symbols that are within specifications.

Batch Printer. A printer which prints documents at a more or less continuous rate. When printing continuously, the hardware cost is relatively unimportant and the cost per document is the main economic factor. A batch printer must be a heavy-duty machine where the hardware cost is justified by the value of all the tasks performed at all the locations to which the documents are addressed.

BCD. *Binary Coded Decimal.* Positional notation in which the individual decimal digits expressing a number in decimal notation are each represented by a binary number.

Bearer Bars. A rectangular bar pattern circumscribing a bar-coded message horizontally and vertically. A bearer bar is employed to provide support for a printing place, usually when printing on corrugated board.

Bidirectional Code. A bar code that permits reading either from left to right or from right to left.

Binary Code. A code which makes use of two distinct characters, usually *0* and *1*.

A code using the binary number system ("powers of two"). In a broad sense, all bar codes are binary, since they use only light and dark areas.

Bit. A one or a zero.

Bit Mapping. A large area can be divided into a grid of smaller areas called pixels. When such a grid is placed over a graphic image, and the presence or absence of a portion of that graphic image is sensed in each pixel, the process is called bit mapping.

Bit-Stream. A continuous stream of ones and zeros.

Black Bar. Bar printed in readable ink.

Blind Ink. Ink which can be seen by the human eye, but which cannot be detected by a scanning device.

Block. A cluster of two or more physical records that are jointly accessed by one machine instruction.

Boustrophedon. Literally, "ox path." A scanning process wherein alternate traverses are oppositely directed, as when a field is plowed.

Byte. A group of bits which together are assigned character significance.

CCD. *Charge-Coupled Device.* A linear array of transductive elements wherein packets of electrons are set in each element as a result of the quantity of light received during an exposure interval, and where these packets are recovered from the array in the form of a pulse-height-modulated electric signal.

Chain. An organization of a data base in which tuples are strung together by means of pointers.

Character. A single number or letter, or a single bar-code character made up of bars and spaces. A human-readable character is a conventional number or letter; a machine-readable character is the equivalent bar code. The machine-readable version is more precisely called a "cipher."

Character Set. The family of characters available for enciphering within a coding scheme.

Check Digit (Check-Sum). A cipher included within a code's overhead, used for error detection.

Cipher. A member of a family of ciphers, wherein each member constitutes a unique symbol which is substituted, on a one-to-one basis for a letter (or other symbol) of an original text. Bar-code ciphers are machine-readable.

Clean. In relation to bar codes, "clean" includes the concept of evenly printed bars as well as dirt-free spaces.

Clear Zone. The blank area around the four sides of a bar-coded message, provided so that other printing will not interfere with reading the code.

Cluster Controller. An instrument including several ports wherein either standard terminals or PIU nonstandard terminals can be addressed by a system in a serial mode.

Code. A system of symbols (letters, numbers, words) used to designate a letter, a number, a phrase, or perhaps a whole sentence or other complete thought.

Code Density. The number of ciphers per inch permitted by code specifications.

CODE-39™. Code name trademarked by Interface Mechanisms. An alphanumeric code. AIM USD-3 for the Uniform Container Symbol (USC/TCS).

Code Width. The total length of a bar-coded message.

Collision. An event caused by two distinct records whose keys hash to the same address.

Component. A bar or space used in composing bar-code ciphers.

Concentrator. An instrument which provides several ports for driving a number of wands, slot readers, and the like from one terminal, and excludes the use of all other similar devices while it has the terminal's attention. A means of prioritizing for an electronic queue may be a feature.

Continuous Code. A bar-coding scheme wherein each cipher ends in a space. That is, the spaces between ciphers are a part of the code.

Contrast. Amount of difference in reflectance between the dark bars and light spaces of a bar code. Measured by PCS (Print Contrast Signal), also called PCR (Print Contrast Ratio).

Cut Sheet. A rectangular piece of paper cut to a specific size.

Data Bank. A collection of data bases.

Data Base. An organized collection of stored data controlled by a specific schema and having a level of controlled redundancy.

Data-Base Administrator. An individual who controls the design and use of a data base.

Data Independence. The property of the logical or physical structure of a data base (schema) that allows the structure to be changed without the application program's view of the data having to be changed.

Data Item. The smallest unit of data that has meaning. Synonymous with "field."

Data Set. A named collection of logically related data items having one of several prescribed arrangements—direct, random, or serial.

Demand Printer. A printer which creates individual documents one at a time, when so directed. In a demand printer the tear-off line must be within a fraction of an inch of the print line to avoid media waste. A demand printer is exposed to light duty where the hardware cost is justified by the value of the tasks performed in the immediate vicinity.

Depth of Field. Maximum spacing of a wand tip above the printed surface, or the dimension between a minimum distance and a maximum distance over which a read head can detect a message printed on a coded surface.

Destruction Protection. Protection of records and equipment. Maximum protection is achieved where the beginning record is held off-line, where the logging equipment (and beginning record) is physically separated from the equipment housing the current record, and where the logging equipment and the current recording equipment have separate power sources.

Direct Data Set. A data set whose records are stored by referring to their relative record addresses through the use of numeric key values.

Discrete Code. A bar code where each cipher begins and ends with a bar. That is, the spaces between ciphers are not a part of the code and so can vary freely. (Cf "Continuous Code.")

Distributed Intelligence. A condition, in a computer-directed system, wherein both memory and processing power are lodged at each data-collecting point.

Document Sophistication. An expression of the quantities of both machine-readable and human-readable data represented by a document, as well as the flexibilities of both format and means of printing.

Dual Orientation. Identical bar-coded messages printed with normal and stacked orientation, so that one can be read regardless of how the label is turned in relation to a read head.

EAN. *European Article Number,* a bar-code system corresponding to the UPC system in the United States. Many scanners can be set up to read both EAN and UPC bar codes.

Electronic Queue. Both a means of prioritizing entry to a computer system, and an electronic means of communicating entry status to an operator in a work station.

Element. The minimum width of bar, and the minimum width of space, which can be printed and detected by a bar-code system. The same as "X."

Elemental Bit. The assignment meaning of "one" to an elemental dark bar, and of "zero" to an elemental light bar.

Emissivity. The amount of electromagnetic radiation, as measured on a per-unit basis, which is emitted from a source.

Emulsion Side. The image-bearing side of a film master. It can be identified visually by the slightly raised image. The nonemulsion side is called the base side.

Emulsion Up. Orientation of a film master when the human-readable numbers and letters read correctly.

Entity. Something about which data is recorded.

Error Rate. Total number of errors per number of readings attempted (or per number of readings accomplished).

Field. The smallest unit of named data. (Data item, data element, elementary item.)

File. Collection of examples of one particular type of data-set tuple.

Film Master. A negative or positive transparency of a specific bar-coded message from which a printing plate is produced.

First Read Rate. The number of correct reads divided by the number of attempted reads.

Flat File. A two-dimensional file (tabulation of tuples).

Font. A specific size and style of printer's type.

Foreign Cut Sheet. A document created outside the control of a central authority.

Format. The physical or geometrical arrangement specified for a particular bar-code symbol.

Frisket. An adhesive label attached to an otherwise deficient document for the purpose of bringing current the information carried by that document.

Graphics. Printed images of any kind which can be evaluated by the human eye.

Graphics Capability. The ability of a printer to print graphic images.

Guard Bars. The tall bars used at the sides and center of UPC and EAN bar-code symbols. They provide reference points for scanning.

The lines, printed along the top and bottom of a bar-coded message, which are designed to abort an angular scan.

Hand Scanning. Use of a hand-held wand or scanner. Portable scanners are important for inventorying, reading shelf labels, etc.

Hashing. A direct-addressing technique that converts a key value into a pseudorandom number from which a record address can be derived.

Header. A message printed at the beginning of a document which uniquely identifies that particular document.

Header Printer. A printer configured so as to print a header on a document when that document is inserted into a slot.

High-Order Number. The most significant number in a bar-coded message. In ''1000,'' the number ''1'' is the high-order number.

Hit. The achievement of an acceptable read in nine or fewer scans of a coded message sample.

Identification. Establishing the identity (so as to maximize security) of human participants by some physical attribute—fingerprint, voice print, palm print, or the like. Otherwise, something known like a password or cipher, and/or something carried like a key or card, must suffice.

Image Orientation. Orientation of the image of a film master; it can be emulsion up or emulsion down.

Individual Pointer. One of two record addresses associated with a transaction for each data set opened by that transaction. The OUT pointer points to the last record stored by the transaction, while the IN pointer points to the last record retrieved by the transaction.

Intercipher Gap. The space between the last bar of one cipher and the first bar of an adjacent cipher of a discrete bar-coded message.

Interleaved Bar Code. A combination in which both black and white bars are significant, but where the black bars relate to one cipher and the white bars to some other cipher.

Interleaved 2 of 5. A compact number-only bar code with two wide components out of five, per character.

Item Code. In the UPC system, the five-digit number that each manufacturer assigns to each of his products. (See Manufacturer Identification Number.)

Jefferson Chart. A number of strips on which the ten numerals (or even the complete alphabet) are printed in column along one end of each strip, and their bar-code cipher equivalents are printed in column along the other end of that same strip. These strips are then laid side by side and each is moved vertically to the others, until the desired multidigit number appears in line across all the strips. The equivalent bar-coded message will then appear in line, at a particular position across the same strips.

Key. One or more data items used to identify or locate a record.

Key Bypass. The process of introducing information to a digital computer or other system without the use of a manually operated keyboard.

Key Memory. A process whereby information generally passes from keyboard directly to computer memory—usually disk memory—and a computer then performs appropriate analysis on the data in memory.

Data Pathing, Inc., was a pioneer in taking terminals out onto the production floor, where those individuals actually performing work could communicate with a computer via a display of some kind and a key pad.

Key Punch. A process whereby a card punch receives its instructions from a manually activated keyboard.

Well through the 1960s, anyone making use of a digital computer had to penetrate the wall surrounding a computer facility where the elite might someday get around to transforming tabulated data into punched card form—if they felt like it.

Key Transformation. The process of mapping a key into an integer, which can be handled arithmetically to determine a record address.

Kipling, R. An early pioneer in defining transaction descriptions.

Label. A descriptive or identifying word or phrase attached to or otherwise associated with an item.

Ladder Code. A bar code printed vertically, with individual bars looking like rungs of a ladder.

Laser Engraver. A device which engraves graphic images directly into the material from which an item is fabricated through the use of the concentrated heat from a laser's beam.

Laser Printer. A printer which makes use of a laser as a printing operator.

Laser Scanner. A bar-code reading device that uses a low-energy laser as the light source.

LED. *Light Emitting Diode.* A semiconducting device which emits electromagnetic radiation over a very restricted band of light as a result of electrical stimulation.

Light Pen. A hand-held scanning wand.

Line Growth. A printing process wherein a printed line is wider than the printer's line because of ink spread.

Link List. A hashed data set containing pointers to detail tuples and—optionally—to master tuples. A link list is the physical implementation of a named relationship.

Log. A sequence of written transaction descriptions.

Log Printer. A printer which reads a bar-coded message preprinted along one edge of a slip or card, and adds a transaction description to that card in the form of a sequentially printed log.

Loop. An association of tuples within one file.

Low-Order Number. When reading a number from left to right, the number farthest to the right.

Magnetic Stripe. Strips of magnetic tape added along one edge of a document—an ID card or whatever.

Magnification Factor. Size of a printed bar code compared to a standard (nominal) size. A magnification factor of 1.00 (= 100%) is nominal size.

Major Key (Match Key). The field or domain over which a named relationship (q.v.)

is defined. In a detail set, the major key enables all record occurrences (tuples) having the same value in that field to be logically grouped.

Manufacturer Identification Number. In the UPC system, the five-digit number assigned to a manufacturer by the Uniform Product Code Council, Inc. This number appears as the left half of the UPC number.

Mapping. A defined correspondence between two sets of values, such as that between a primary key and a storage address.

Matte. A dull surface. The characteristics of a surface with a high degree of spectral dispersion. A surface which cannot reflect an image.

Message. A finite string of ciphers which carry a complete unit of information. Same as "word" or "symbol."

Message Length. The number of useful ciphers contained in a single coded message.

MICR. *Magnetic Ink Character Recognition.* A technology for encoding numbers on checks with magnetic ink.

Mil. One-thousandth of an inch (0.001 inch) or approximately 0.0254 mm.

Minor Key. The least significant sort field in a detail tuple.

Misread. A bad read or substitution error.

Module. The same as "element." The smallest width of bars or spaces in a bar code. In the UPC system, each character contains 7 modules and each bar or space can have a width of 1, 2, 3, or 4 modules.

Modulo Check Digit (Check Cipher). The specific check cipher used in a bar code. It signals the scanner if an error has been made in reading.

Move Ticket. A document printed on the factory floor which, when associated with an item, indicates the location to which that item should next be directed.

Moving Beam Reader. A code reader that searches for a ciphered message by sweeping a moving beam of light through a field.

MRP. *Material Resource Planning.* The computer-aided art of causing an item of interest to arrive at a particular location within a very narrow time frame.

MRU. *Multiple Reader Unit.* An instrument which includes a number of PIUs in one package, wherein several nonstandard terminals can be addressed by the system in a parallel mode.

Named Relationship. A specification that defines groupings of related detail tuples and, optionally, associates each group with a master tuple.

NDC. *National Drug Code.* The Related Items Code: ten digit code numbers administered by the U.S. Food and Drug Administration, expressed in the UPC barcode symbol. These numbers use the number system character *3* as the first digit, rather than the *0* used by regular supermarket items.

Negative. A film master negative, having black and clear (white) areas reversed, compared to the final bar code, in which the background will be black and the human-readable numbers white.

Network Structure. A ranked relationship among record types such that the highest level in the network has only one record type, called a root, and all record types except the root are related to at least one record type on a higher level than themselves.

Nominal Size. The standard size for a bar-code symbol. Most codes can be used over a range of magnifications, say from 0.80 to 1.20 of nominal. (See Magnification Factor.)

Nonread. Absence of data output after an operator has scanned a machine-readable label.

Normal Bar Code. A bar code printed in an orientation giving the visual effect of a picket fence.

Not Quite Flat File. An alternate-valued field in an otherwise flat file.

Number System Character. The first (left-hand) digit in a UPC number; it identifies different number systems. Regular items carry a *0;* drug (NDC/HRI) items carry a *3;* random weight items have a *2.*

Numeric Bar Code. A code consisting only of ciphers representing numeric data, possibly with a few additional symbols.

Nybble. A meaningful group of bits smaller than a byte.

OCR. *Optical Character Recognition.* The process whereby human-readable characters are read by instrumented means.

OCR-A. A font designed for maximum machine readability.

OCR-B. A specific style of letters and numbers used for the human-readable characters specified for use with the UPC, EAN, and UCS/TCS bar-code symbols.

OCR Ink. Carbon ink (or ink which can be read by infrared scan).

Omnidirectional. Able to read a bar-code symbol from any angle. Supermarket checkout laser scanners are omnidirectional; as long as the bar code passes over the scanner window, it can be read, regardless of how it is turned.

Operation. A unit of work. The process whereby a work piece is changed from one state to some other state.

Out Pointer. The relative byte address of the last record stored.

Overhead. The fixed amount of a bar-code message consumed in the START/STOP, message checking, and (in some codes) character-set designator ciphers.

Packing Density. A measure of the amount of information which can be placed in a unit area or (in the case of bar codes) along a unit line.

Page. A block of data that can be located in main or secondary memory.

Page Reader. An instrument which can read pages of information printed in an OCR font. These cannot be used to read labels on any other item.

Panache. A characteristic of the means by which an MIS system is successfully implemented on the factory floor. It means to go first class, with aggressive elegance, exaggeration, verve, and style.

Parity. System for encoding ciphers as "odd" or "even" bar-code patterns. Not related to whether the original number is odd or even. Used to provide a self-checking feature in bar codes.

Parity Bar (Parity Bit, Parity Module). In various bar-code systems, a specific arrangement to provide self-checking.

Participative Traveler. A traveler which includes labels within its format which can be peeled off and affixed to other items as the traveler moves from work station to work station.

Path Record. A record occurrence in a link list that contains, in time or minor key sequence, pointers to the associated details. If a master has been defined, a path record also contains a pointer to the master tuple.

Percent Decode. The number of times a message is read per 100 scans performed by a laser scanner.

Percent Successful Reading Rate. Scan rate minus error rate, divided by scan rate, times one hundred.

Personal Terminal. A work-station terminal. A terminal used exclusively by one operator.

Physical. An adjective that refers to the form in which data or systems exist in reality.

PIU. *Peripheral Interface Unit.* An instrument which provides an interface between a system designed to serve a number of standard terminals, and a nonstandard terminal. It makes the nonstandard look standard to the system.

Pixel. "Picture element." When the area occupied by a graphic image is divided into a grid of smaller areas, each of the smaller areas is called a "pixel."

Plex. Hierarchal node structure (one parent per node) where the nodes are fields, segments, or tuples.

Pointer. Address of one tuple, contained within another tuple and used by a program accessing the former when retrieving the latter.

Poor Man's Header Printer. A stamp consisting of a number of rubber belts upon which a family of bar-code ciphers is raised. The belts may be rotated independently to allow any message to be printed which is possible from the cipher set supported.

POS. Often used as shorthand for a *Point-of-Sale* data-entry system, such as supermarket laser scanner checkouts.

Positive. A film master positive, having black and white (clear) areas in the same relationship as in the final printed bar code, in which the background will be white and the human-readable characters will be black.

Preprinted Bar Codes. A bar code printed on a label, for later application to a package or other container. This simplifies maintaining printing tolerances, when the package substrate is difficult to print on directly.

Primary Key. A key unique to one tuple (entity identifier).

Printability Gauge. A printer's tool used to determine the amount of print gain under given printing conditions.

Printability Range. Range of print gain found under actual working conditions, based upon press sheets selected at random during a press run.

Print Contrast. Comparison of reflectivity between bars and spaces.

A comparison between the reflectances of an ink printed on a background and that background.

Print Gain. Gain in bar width in the final printed bar-code symbol, compared to the original precision film master. Influenced by plate-making and ink spread during printing. Film masters are made with an appropriate amount of bar width reduction to allow for print gain.

Production Control. The art of merging hierarchies of authority, skill, process, configuration, function, time, and space into one interrelated system of productivity.

In a manufacturing community, the department responsible for creating and maintaining such a system.

PROM. *Programmable Read Only Memory.*

Quiet Zone. The area immediately preceding the START cipher and following the STOP cipher, which contains no marking.

Qwerty Keyboard. The commonly used, familiar typewriter keyboard.

Read Acceptance Probability. The number of hits divided by the number of samples scanned.

Read Area. Area covered by a scanner. Especially important in material-handling applications, as when scanners read cartons on a conveyer belt. Bar codes must reliably pass through the read area.

Read Integrity. The number of correct reads divided by the number probability of hits.

Read Reliability. The combination of a high first read rate and a low substitution error rate.

Reconstruction. The re-creation of a current data base by adding logged information to the beginning record. This should be feasible at any time.

Record. A group of related data items treated as a unit.

Record Addressing. The means of locating data in storage and subsequently retrieving them on the basis of a key.

Reflectance. Amount of light reflected back from a surface. Reflectance is measured under specified conditions in which a surface coated with barium sulfate is considered to be a perfect diffuse reflector of light. (Diffuse reflection scatters light in all directions.) Various instruments are available to measure reflectance directly.

The fraction of the total radiant energy incident upon a surface which is reflected.

Relation. A flat file, a two-dimensional array of data items.

Resolution. The dimension of the smallest code element that can be printed by a bar-code printer or identified by a bar-code reader; or the larger of these two, when discussing a bar-code system in general.

In optics, sharpness, ability to reproduce fine detail, ability of a scanner to read narrow bars in bar codes. In printing, measurement of the narrowest bar that can be printed satisfactorily.

ROM. *Read Only Memory.*

Scan. Movement of a scanner light beam over a bar code (or of the bar code past the light beam).

Scan Area. Same as read area: the area covered by a scanner.

Scanner. Device that converts bar-code symbols to electrical signals for data input and storage.

A device used to read and identify a pattern of coded information.

Used interchangeably with "reader."

Scanning Range. Maximum distance at which a scanner can read bar codes. Equal to optical throw plus depth of field.

Scanning Wand. A hand-held scanning device connected to a data-input or storage device.

Scan Rate. Total number of scans per unit of time.

Schema. The structure of a data base.

Scob. A pattern defect.

Secondary Key. A key shared by a tuple family. It may be a primary key of some other file.

Segment. Collection of multiple fields found within a tuple which operate together as a unit and which is given a name (aggregate, group item, etc.).

Self-checking (code). A code using a checking algorithm which can be applied to each cipher to guard against undetected errors. Non-self-checking codes employ a check digit or other redundancy in addition to the data message.

Self-clocking (code). A code designed for reading with a single-aperture reader over a range of velocities, with reasonable allowance for change in velocity after a reading has commenced.

SER. *Substitution Error Rate.* The number of incorrect readings as a percentage of the total number of readings obtained.

Set. A two-level tree of tuples.

SEUGO. *Significant End Use Goal Orientation.* Indicates the use of information coded in a label whereby that information is used to direct a transaction.

Shop Ticket Printer. A printer used for demand printing of small documents such as move-tickets, labels, etc.

Skin Sheet. A document covering a stack of documents which carries an abstract of the information supplied by the other documents.

Slip Printer. A demand printer which does not include a source of print media. Rather, small cut sheets (slips) are introduced by hand for each print cycle.

Slot Reader. An instrument which reads a machine-readable header from a document when that document is drawn through a slot.

Sort Key. A key used for determining the access sequence of records in a data set.

Space. The lighter element of a bar code.

Spectral Response. Sensitivity of a scanner or other device to different colors of light. Lasers used in laser scanners generally operate in the red part of the spectrum, which affects the colors that can be used for printing scannable bar codes.

Specular Reflection. Mirror-like reflection that occurs at a specified angle. Shiny surfaces producing specular reflections may cause problems for bar-code scanners.

Stacked Bar Code. A bar code printed in an orientation giving the visual effect of a ladder.

Start Cipher/Stop Cipher. A bar-code representing "beginning of code" or "end of code." It also indicates to the scanner whether the code is being read backward and should be reversed.

Straight Bar Code. One in which the white spaces between black bars are not a part of the code.

Stroke. Thickness of a bar.

Substitution Error Rate. A quantification of the condition which exists when an attempt to read a cipher results in a wrong conclusion—a wrong reading. The rate at which a substitution error occurs is an important system criterion, as it measures the quality of information held in a data base.

The number of incorrect reads divided by the number of successful reads.

Substrate. The material or medium upon which bar codes are printed.

Symbol. Combination of all necessary bar-code ciphers to form a complete data message; data, START/STOP, and check digits.

Symbol Density. Amount of data contained per inch in a bar-code symbol. Limited by the width of the narrowest bar or space.

Tamper-Proof. The quality of particular software packages which makes it relatively difficult for an innovative programmer to bypass controls.

Task. A basic unit of work.

Ticket Printer. A printer which can print small documents such as tickets, tags, labels, and the like.

Time-Sequential. An adjective referring to a chronological or serial order.

Tote Box. A container commonly used in various discrete manufacturing activities which contains the materials—parts and documents—necessary to complete an operation or series of operations.

Transaction Validation. The conformity of a transaction to certain preestablished definitions determined by software. Without such validation, no transaction can be processed.

Transducer. A device which converts a physical phenomenon of interest (pressure, temperature, flow, electromagnetic radiation, and the like) into an electric analog in the form of voltage, current, or frequency magnitudes.

Transport Case Symbol. European equivalent to the UCS (Uniform Container Symbol) for shipping containers.

Traveler. A documentary means of communicating the intentions of a central authority to a number of operators in dispersed work stations. Travelers move with the work pieces from work station to work station.

Truncation. Decreasing the length of the bars in a bar-code symbol below the normal specification. Truncation decreases a symbol's ability to be read omnidirectionally and should be avoided.

Tuple. A group of related fields (of various formats and various lengths) used to describe an entity. (A "row" relationship in a multicolumn tabulation—i.e., the information found in a Hollerith card.) Only one unique tuple is allowed in any data bank (record).

UCS. *Uniform Container Symbol.* Bar-code message designed for printing on corrugated shipping containers; result of Distribution Symbology Study Group.

Unary Link. A connection that associates tuples in a single relation and provides partially defined ordering of the tuples.

UPC. *Universal Product Code.* A ten-digit code number that identifies a wide range of products and their manufacturers; printed as the UPC symbol (bar code) on packages.

UPCC. *Uniform Product Code Council.* Organization responsible for overseeing and administering the Universal Product Code.

USD. *Uniform Symbol Description.* Specifications set up by AIM (Automatic Identification Manufacturers) for bar-code standards.

USD–1. Interleaved 2/5.

USD–2. Subset CODE–39. The strongest possible alphanumeric code.

USD–3. CODE–39 (Trademark of Interface Mechanisms, Inc.). It includes four out-of-pattern ciphers.

USD–4. CODABAR.

Version A, Version E. Version A is the standard UPC bar-code symbol. Version E is a special shortened version, requiring less space, formed by use of zero suppression.

Void. White or light area in a bar caused by printing error. It can cause a bar to scan as a space.

Wand. A penlike hand-held device used to read bar codes by passing its tip over the printed marks and transmitting optically obtained message data for electronic decode. It is sometimes called a light-pen, but this term is easily confused with the light-pens used as curser controls for CRT terminals.

Wand Reader. A hand-held device operated by movement over the area to be read.

Word. A complete "thought" as indicated by a combination of characters or their equivalent bar-code ciphers. Same as "symbol."

Work Center. A point from which the activities of a number of work stations are controlled.

Work Order. The authorization to perform an increment of work.

Work Station. A location where work is actually performed.

"X." The minimum width of bar, or space, which can be printed with integrity when using a given printing process.

Index